A Visible Wound

Julie Friedeberger was born in New York in 1935. She moved to England in 1961 and worked for many years in publishing. Since 1987 she has devoted herself to teaching and writing about yoga which she has practised since 1970. She is the author of *Office Yoga* and she writes regularly for yoga magazines. She lives in Blackheath, London, with her husband, the painter Klaus Friedeberger.

A
Visible
Wound

A Healing Journey
Through Breast Cancer

Julie Friedeberger

*with practical and spiritual guidance
for women, their partners and families*

vega

First published by Element Books Ltd 1996
© Vega 2002
Text © Julie Friedeberger 1996

ISBN 1-84333-359-7

A catalogue record for this book is available
from the British Library

Published in 2002 by
Vega
64 Brewery Road
London, N7 9NT

A member of Chrysalis Books plc

Visit our website at www.chrysalisbooks.co.uk

Printed in Great Britain
by Lightning Source
Cover designed by Design Revolution, Brighton

Dedication

For my husband, Klaus, and my teacher,
Swami Dharmānanda Saraswati

*Whoever has helped us to a larger understanding
is entitled to our gratitude for all time.*
Norman Douglas

and for my surgeon, Alan Stoker

Surgery too is God-given
Swami Dharmānanda Saraswati

Acknowledgements

No one comes through cancer without help. Without the generous support of many friends, I certainly couldn't have; nor could I have written this book. My deepest thanks and love go to everyone who helped me.

Klaus, my husband, has been my rock through breast cancer, as he has been through our life together. I thank him not only for his love and support, but for his firm, unflinching, clear-sighted grasp of the realities of life, which have made it easier for me to look straight at them.

Swami Dharmānanda Saraswati, my teacher, has given me the spiritual guidance I needed to meet the experience of cancer, as always in her own unique, down-to-earth, practical, ever-helpful way. No words can ever express my gratitude to her (luckily, Swamiji knows none are needed!).

Alan Stoker's unfailing kindness and compassion have inspired my trust and encouraged me from our first meeting; I am grateful not only for his skill as a surgeon but for his healing presence in my life.

I am also grateful to Alan Thompson, my General Practitioner, for referring me so quickly and decisively for specialist treatment.

Shobhna Chandaria, Annie Calverley, Tania Pemberton, Clare Harrison, Koye Balogun, Caroll Graham and Stella Cooper took over my yoga classes while I recovered from surgery and came to terms with cancer. They gave me the time to heal, and much more; I thank them for their staunch support and friendship.

Lynne Nixon had her mastectomy a year before me; her steady, no-nonsense voice on the telephone talked me through the anticipatory stage of mine. My students, my friends, and my fellow-members of the Dharma Yoga Centre wrote to me, telephoned me, thought about me and prayed for me. They all helped pull me through diagnosis, surgery and recovery to healing, and I thank them.

Kate Clements, bless her, was the first to tell me that it's all right to be single-breasted. I thank her for this, and for all the years of friendship.

Zena Schofield's expert physiotherapy restored me to full-range movement after my mastectomy more quickly than I would have thought possible. I am grateful to her; and to Peter Harrison, who in telling me what I needed to hear at the right moment, restored me to stillness.

Elizabeth Gray was the first to read the book in typescript, and her warm enthusiasm for it was encouraging. My grateful thanks to her, and to Ailsa Fabian, Anne Charvet and John Baldock, my editor at Element Books, for the constructive suggestions which have helped to make it a better, more useful book.

Jane Sill, editor of *Yoga and Health*, started the book off by asking me to write the series of articles, *Reflections on Cancer and Healing*, from which it has grown; I thank her for her interest, her confidence and her support.

I am grateful to Kirsten Wormald for enhancing the book with her drawings for Chapters 8 and 10, and for her wonderful shiatsu treatments.

Vin and Peter Rendel offered me a quiet space in which to do my final revisions, so my last look at the book was in the magical, peaceful surroundings of Hourne Farm during a memorable week of retreat.

The Bristol Cancer Help Centre kindly provided the addresses of the cancer help agencies in the United States, Canada, Australia and New Zealand. I am grateful to them, and to the Cancer Research Campaign and the Thames Cancer Registry for providing breast cancer statistics for these countries.

Contents

Foreword

Breast cancer is a worldwide epidemic that kills hundreds of thousands of women every year. In the United Kingdom alone there are now around 30,000 new cases every year and 15,000 deaths. The statistics for the United States and Canada, Australia and New Zealand are horrifying too, some of them more so.

In the autumn of 1993 I discovered a lump in my breast, was diagnosed with breast cancer and had a mastectomy. At the time I knew almost nothing about this outrageous disease that has such a multitude of causes and destroys so many lives. I know a lot more now, but I am not an 'expert', and this is not a source book or reference book. Although it touches on the wider issues (which are fundamentally political: I believe that breast cancer is at least partly, perhaps even largely, a preventable disease, and that serious, major research into its possible causes is urgently needed) A Visible Wound is essentially the story of my own healing from breast cancer.

It tells of an inner journey that has transformed my life, a journey that has taken me from disbelief and terror to acknowledgement and acceptance of things as they are, of life as it is. It tells my 'story', but it does more than that. As a student and teacher of yoga, I knew that this ancient, holistic art, which nourished and upheld me as I coped with the most devastating experience of my life, could help others, too. The book shares my knowledge of some of the simple yoga breathing and relaxation techniques that helped me, and I hope that these will be useful to others as they go through the experience of cancer.

I would not have chosen to have cancer, but having it has taught me so much that I would not want to turn the clock back. Cancer has not been a misfortune for me, but a God-given opportunity for spiritual growth and transformation, and I believe that it can be so for others. Grave illness does not have to be the end; it can be the beginning. Illness can be understood, and used, as a stepping-stone to healing and as a path to a deeper knowledge of death and life.

I did not start out with this understanding: it developed as I moved towards a clearer awareness of what the cancer experience was really about for me, and as I took responsibility for my healing. In this, my yoga practice and my knowledge of yoga philosophy and psychology guided and supported me. How they did so is woven into the narrative – I hope in such a way as to give useful insight to others who are working their way through to their own healing.

Breast cancer happens not only to the woman who gets it, but also to everyone who is close to her. *A Visible Wound* is therefore not just for women, but for their husbands, partners and families as well. I hope it will also be read by the doctors, nurses and practitioners involved in their care. Others – men as well as women – who have other kinds of cancers, or other serious illnesses, or who are undergoing other life crises such as bereavement, may also find the book useful.

Shock and grief, anger and despair, fear of pain and death are the common experience of all who face an illness that puts life on the line. These strong, often violent emotions are themselves frightening, and denial is a common – and understandable – response to them. *A Visible Wound* suggests how these emotions can be handled and their energy transformed.

Denial leads directly to repression, which traps our precious energy and gives our buried emotions even more power over us. But if we were to let them come to the surface and stand back from them a little, if we could learn to observe and acknowledge them, we would begin to gain clarity on them, and they would lose their power over us. Instead of getting 'stuck' in denying them, we would transcend them.

This is all part of the healing journey. It is a long, ongoing, often difficult journey, but a therapeutic, endlessly interesting, ultimately transformative one. For a while it claims our full attention, and for this we need to give ourselves time – time for the 'secret miracles' within us to come forth.

Finishing this book and handing it over to its readers, two years after the discovery of my lump, is not the end of my journey: I am on it still. Others who undertake it will discover that there are great rewards, great truths and great joy to be found along the way. I wish us all well on the journey, and may God's blessings always be with us.

Julie Friedeberger

Prologue
'They Make You a New One'

Wednesday 10 November, 1993. In her tiny, bare, upstairs consulting room in the Harmony Chinese Medicine clinic in the Leytonstone High Road, Northeast London, Dr Lin felt my lump and my armpit.

I was there for acupuncture to boost my immune system for the ordeal that I already knew lay ahead. I had not yet been 'officially' diagnosed, and my consultant's '90 per cent certainty' that my lump was breast cancer left a margin of hope for a miracle – but really I knew. I hadn't yet consciously acknowledged what I knew, but in the next few moments Dr Lin was to help me do that.

Dr Lin spoke very little English. But she made herself very clear. 'You must go hospital. Have operation. Quickly!' Then, making a slicing motion at my breast, she said, 'They cut *here*'; and, aiming another slice at my armpit, 'and *here*'. I swallowed. 'All off?' 'Yes!' she said, nodding emphatically. And saw my face, and grinned an impish grin. 'Doesn't matter!' she said cheerfully. 'They make you a new one.'

I drove home in tears, wretched and furious, wishing desperately that I hadn't come, that I hadn't had to sustain that brutal blow that had pushed my lurking knowledge and all my fears to the surface. But it was salutary, and I soon came to be grateful to Dr Lin for delivering it, because in that moment I took in the reality of mastectomy. Two days later, when I returned to the hospital for the results of my tests, I was ready to hear what the consultant had to say to me. Dr Lin's bombshell had presented me with a fact, with a bit of reality, and I took it in and accepted it.

Ten days earlier, on Monday 1 November, I had gone to see my General Practitioner with a lump in my left breast, and had been referred immediately to a consultant breast surgeon, whom I saw at Greenwich District Hospital on Friday the 5th. On Friday 12 November Alan Stoker gave me his diagnosis of breast cancer, and on Friday 19 November he removed my left breast and nineteen lymph nodes.

Those nineteen days were my initiation into an experience that would, I knew even then, alter everything for me. Somehow I knew that my life would now change, and that I would not ever again be the same as I had been. The tremendous jolt of knowing I had cancer pushed me from where I was – a safe, secure place where I was living a challenging, rewarding life as a yoga teacher and writer, contentedly married for over thirty years to the husband I love – into a hinterland of terror and despair, a place which seemed, just then, to hold nothing but grief and desolation. There would be no going back from that place of anguish; I could only go forward. But how?

One woman in 12 in Britain can expect to get breast cancer in the course of a lifetime; in America 1 in 10. I imagine that most women, knowing the statistics, fear breast cancer and wonder how they would cope if it ever happened to them. This is natural and rational, and may even prove helpful in the event. But I had never given it so much as a passing thought. This wasn't because I had stuck my head in the sand (although it may sound as if I had); it was because I had never had to be concerned about my health. It had always been excellent, it had never stopped me doing anything I wanted to do, and if I thought about it at all it was simply to assume that it would last me until I died at some very old age, which (however old I got as life unfolded!) was of course a long way away. Cancer was something that happened to other people.

But now I had breast cancer. Here it was, a fact, staring me in the face. I was seriously ill. I might die soon. Even if I recovered and lived for many more years, I would never again be able to take my health for granted. Whatever happened, my life was now about to be turned upside down. I was going to have to stop doing what I was doing and deal with cancer. This knowledge literally pulled the ground from under my feet.

It had taken me a long time to get my feet on firm ground. Only six years earlier, at the age of 52, I had changed direction. After working in publishing for over 30 years – first in the United States where I was born and grew up, and then in Britain where I came in 1961 to live and to marry Klaus (we had met in Florence, Italy, the year before) – I had begun what I considered the real work of my life. I had practised yoga for nearly twenty years when I started teaching classes in 1987. My own teacher, Swami Dharmānanda Saraswati, had encouraged me, first to start teaching and, later on, to train teachers. In 1990, at 55, I took early retirement from publishing to devote my time and my energy to teaching and writing about yoga.

From the first lesson I gave, teaching yoga was the most satisfying thing I had ever done: personally satisfying because I loved doing it, but ultimately satisfying because I wasn't doing it for myself; it was helping others. I was teaching four weekly classes, and running a teacher training course for a group of keen students who were themselves now starting to teach. I had published a book, *Office Yoga*, the fruit of my 30 years' experience at a desk, and of applying yoga to all the tensions and stresses of the work situation. I was writing regularly for yoga magazines. Life was good, evolving as it should, continually presenting me with new challenges, new responsibilities, new joys. Suddenly, it all had to stop. It was all going to change, and I dreaded that prospect.

To my astonishment, what happened was that the change I feared so much ceased to be a threat and turned into a blessing. Before long I came to see it not as menacing, but as positive and nourishing, as a healing transformation of all that I do and think and am.

A Visible Wound tells the story of how this happened, of the therapeutic process by which I moved from that place of fear and despair to a place of greater strength and faith and understanding than I had ever known before. It is about my healing, about my inner journey from the shock and dismay I felt at the prospect of losing a breast, to acceptance: acceptance of my wound and my 'flat side', acceptance of things as they are. It has taken me from the grief and terror that overwhelmed me on realizing that I was seriously ill and might die sooner that I had expected to, to a deeper knowledge of the meaning of illness and the reality of death – and, therefore, of life.

I had only one reason for wanting to write and publish a book about my experience: to help other women with breast cancer (or anyone with any life-threatening illness) and their partners, families and carers, to see how the experience of illness can be used as a unique opportunity for spiritual growth and transformation. I thought that if I could find a way of sharing the process by which I made the profound shift from denial to acceptance, from terror to equanimity, it might help others to achieve it too. Much of what I have written is 'recollected in tranquillity', but I have also chosen some of the most candid extracts from the journal I kept during the year following my diagnosis, which convey the clearest idea of the process as I went through it.

As I worked on the book, two objectives, equally important, became clear.

The first was to relate my experience truthfully in the hope that the approach and attitudes that have so far brought me through cancer, and the perspective I have acquired on the issues that arise when serious illness threatens life, may give others insight that will help them.

The other was to share with my readers, in clear and simple terms that can be put to use by anyone, some of the basic yoga breathing, relaxation and meditation techniques that I have practised and taught for years, and which helped me to hold my balance throughout the most extreme and daunting crisis I have ever had to face.

Everyone who develops cancer, or any other serious illness, will of course meet that life-altering experience in their own way, and find their own way through it. The personal reflections I am sharing here may not be relevant for everyone. But I hope that those who read them will find them useful as they work their way through to their healing.

My own healing has been grounded in yoga, which for many years has nourished and shaped my life. Yoga is not solely, or even primarily, an exercise system; it is a holistic practice for bringing about balance and harmony on all the levels of our being. Practising yoga develops the steadiness and inner strength that enable us to cope with all the obstacles that are put in our path, and to use them as stepping-stones to greater knowledge and deeper awareness. This was how it had always worked for me. So when I knew I had cancer, I expected that all I had learned would come to my aid, and it did. Without yoga, my experience of cancer would have been very different.

A Visible Wound is more than just my personal story; I hope it will give real practical as well as spiritual help to others who find themselves facing the painful realities of cancer. It tells exactly how yoga helped me, and how it can help others. These aspects are an integral part of the narrative, and there are also two chapters wholly devoted to the breathing, relaxation and meditation techniques that have been so useful to me, with clear instructions for them.

They are simple techniques for steadying, calming and focusing our minds, concentrating and conserving our energy, and increasing our strength and stability. They help us to release tension and deal with stress, to draw our scattered forces together and centre ourselves. I have practised and taught them for years; practising them has helped me through all the ups and downs of daily living, and in teaching them I have seen how they have helped others. When I discovered I had cancer they proved their worth a hundred-fold. They helped me to hold my balance under the onslaught of emotions that began to assail me within minutes of leaving my doctor's surgery. They helped me to acknowledge, observe, accept and release those emotions. And they have helped me work my way through every stage of the experience since – diagnosis, surgery, recovery, coming-to-terms and healing – and to integrate into my changing life the learning implicit in each stage.

These techniques are easy to learn and to use; anyone can practise them. Some involve body movement, but none demands physical suppleness or fitness. Nor do they require a great deal of time, but if you enjoy them and find them helpful you will probably want to return to them periodically throughout your day. They will help you to defuse tension and let go of anxiety, and to concentrate your powers of attention on the challenges that lie before you: to look clearly and steadily at what is happening to you; to conserve your energy and direct it towards your healing; and to create an internal environment conducive to the working of your innate healing powers.

Healing happens on all levels of our being, from the spiritual to the physical. Women who have had breast surgery will find in Chapter 10 a series of exercises to help restore full movement to the arm and shoulder, and some guidance on scar management.

A cancer diagnosis is not, necessarily, a death sentence. Most of us are aware by now that not everyone who gets cancer dies of it; many people recover and live productive lives for many years. But the threat is there, and chilling to contemplate. Suddenly our health, which we may always have taken for granted, is no longer a sure thing. Suddenly, although we may not feel even slightly ill, we have a serious illness, for which all the current medical treatments are drastic. Suddenly, we are facing the possibility of an earlier death than we had expected, and the wrenching knowledge that we may have to leave friends, partners, children, behind, and leave unfinished the work we came here to do.

Suddenly, we are confronting our mortality, and however well we knew, or thought we knew, that nobody lives forever, this new level of realization is a different matter altogether. Somehow, we have to find a way of coming to grips with all the overwhelming emotions that a cancer diagnosis unleashes. Predominant amongst these for most people are fear, anger and grief.

The old saying 'The only thing we have to fear is fear itself' isn't just a meaningless cliché. Fear *is* frightening. So is anger. So is grief. So is every strong, intense emotion. The natural inclination we may feel to suppress these frightening emotions can lead us to deny them altogether, especially if our upbringing has schooled us to cope on our own, not to grumble or ask others for help, and to keep our real feelings hidden.

Keeping our feelings hidden from others can be a valid choice for some, though it happens not to be for me. But whether or not we share them with others, it is better that we don't hide them from ourselves. Being truthful to ourselves and acknowledging our fear, anger and grief, is a way through those feelings, a way through to understanding and acceptance. Letting our feelings in is an important step on the path to healing.

The rising of a wave of fear can in itself be terrifying, and our immediate impulse may be to duck it, to grasp at a distraction, like watching television, or eating or drinking something, or throwing ourself into a job to 'take our mind off it'. Sometimes this is appropriate: for example, we may need to hold our emotions at a distance during working hours in order to do our job adequately. There is no danger in this as long as we are aware of the feelings and realize that we are putting them to one side for the moment, for a purpose. But if our 'fear of fear' leads us to deny our feelings, if we habitually refuse to admit them into consciousness, a store of suppressed emotions will accumulate which will require all our energy simply to keep it suppressed. That is a waste of precious energy. That way lie depression, exhaustion, increased stress and the consequent impaired functioning of the immune system – the last things anyone with cancer needs.

Emotions gain strength when we resist acknowledging them. But if we could understand that they are only emotions and not dangerous weapons of destruction; if we could understand that they are not 'us'; if we could turn towards them instead of away from them, own them instead of repulsing them, let them enter into consciousness and look at them instead of stuffing them back down whenever they threaten to surface, we would be able to see them for what they are: 'just feelings'.

When we do this, when we look at our feelings and own them and accept them as they are, they begin to lose their power over us. Eventually, they pass: they dissolve, and we can let go of them.

Of course, looking at our emotions is feasible only if we can keep them from knocking us right over. By this I do not mean blocking or suppressing them; I mean letting them arise but detaching ourselves from them, standing back a little from them and not getting so involved in them.

When emotions do threaten to overwhelm us, we need techniques to help us stand back a little, so that we *can* look at them. The breathing and relaxation exercises in Chapters 8 and 9 helped me to hold my balance, and to go through the experience with my eyes and heart open.

Writing this, knowing that many will read it who have had cancer or who have it now, and whose experience has perhaps been even more painful than mine, or who may be enduring it alone, I am very aware of how fortunate I have been, how blessed, with the love and support of my husband, friends, teacher and students, and with my surgeon and his skilled, swift, caring treatment. Mastectomy surgery is no picnic, but I recovered quickly from it, and as I wasn't considered to need radiation or chemotherapy afterwards I was able to direct my thoughts and energies to healing, without having to cope with the stress of further drastic treatments which might have produced unpleasant side-effects.

(My follow-up treatment was tamoxifen, the anti-oestrogen drug now usually given to post-menopausal women instead of chemotherapy. I have had no problems with it, apart from a tendency to put on weight more easily and to overheat during hot summers.)

When I was told that a mastectomy was the best way of dealing with my 3 ¹/₂ centimetre lump, more likely than a lumpectomy to avoid local recurrence, I felt instantly that if there was to be nothing worse for me to go through, losing a breast would be a small price to pay for my life. Two years on, I know it was. And sometimes, when I talk or write about the knowledge and insight cancer has given me, I wonder if it seems that I have come by it easily, that compared to others who have suffered more, I have so far got off lightly.

I don't say this to belittle my own experience but simply to be clear about its limits, and to explain why, not having experienced radiation or chemotherapy, I don't speak on these subjects. This isn't another information book about breast cancer; I am not competent to write such a book, and besides, many other writers have done so. It is a narrative of my own journey, a sharing of my own experience. To those whose journey has been more difficult than mine, or who have had to go through it without the support I have had, I can offer only what I know, in the sincere hope that it will help them through their own trials.

I discovered my lump in October. As soon as I went to the doctor with it, I was sure that something big, something important was happening. I felt exactly as I had as a child when embarking on a roller-coaster ride: that long, slow, ominous, tugging pull up the hill before the first stomach-turning descent and all the subsequent peaks and valleys. I knew it would be vital for me to keep in touch with myself, to tell myself the truth, to keep myself centred and not let myself get swamped or scattered. If I was going on a roller-coaster ride I wanted to drive, or at least sit up front so I could see what was happening: I didn't want to be dragged along behind.

I started my journal.

> **Thursday 4 November 1993**
> In the shower this morning I suddenly thought of keeping a journal. Perhaps it will be of help to others in the future, and it may be of help to me now. The experience that I have just begun is an important one, whatever happens, however it ends, and I feel it is important to record it as it develops.
>
> I mean to learn from it whatever it has to teach me.
>
> Clare said 'Soon it will be Friday and then you'll know more: the worst thing is the waiting and not knowing.' That's what I thought at first too; it seemed a long wait from Monday when I saw Alan Thompson to Friday when I have the hospital appointment. But in fact the time has been useful. I have been able to adjust somewhat to the knowledge that something may be seriously wrong, and to look. That's all I can do now, and it has been good to have the time to do it: to look at all the possibilities.
>
> That it is 'nothing' (a simple cyst, a 'benign' growth)
> That it is 'something' (breast cancer)
> That it is something really very bad:
> > breast cancer requiring a full mastectomy
> > breast cancer that has already spread, requiring chemotherapy
> > breast cancer that has spread so far that it cannot be halted and that I may die soon.
>
> There is no way of knowing. Sometimes I think the fact that I feel well, strong, healthy, no different from before, means that I can't be 'seriously ill'. Pam said, 'stay positive', but I don't want to be positive or negative at this point, only clear. I only want to look.

Writing my journal, like my yoga practices, helped me to 'look'. It was therapeutic, of course, but it was more than that: it developed into a kind of meditation practice, a way of giving myself the time and space to identify my feelings and thoughts and draw them out for inspection and observation, which is just what meditation does. When I wrote, in that first entry, 'I mean to learn from it whatever it has to teach me', I was committing myself to a long process, and I knew it. Of that continuing process, the journal has been the mainstay. It has enabled me to observe myself and the shifting landscape of my life, to reach out and catch the issues as they arise, and look at the feelings associated with them.

The ever-present issue for me has been acceptance: acceptance of things as they are, of myself as I am now, of my changed body, of the future and whatever it holds, of reality, of 'the thing as it is'. What is happening is happening; it is as it is. As the Chinese proverb says, 'The rice is boiled.' Once cooked it cannot be changed; it is eaten or it is discarded.

We all have to discover the truth of this in our own time and deal with it in our own way, and having cancer gives it a particular intensity. But there is an aspect of breast cancer that sets it apart from most other kinds of cancer. If a mastectomy is performed it leaves a visible wound, for the woman and everyone close to her to come to terms with.

That visibility has been a help to me.

When Dr Lin said 'All off!' and 'Doesn't matter, they make you a new one,' she was right about what needed to be done, and she was right that it didn't matter. It doesn't, though not for the reason she thought. As it turned out, it did not take me very long to accept the loss of my breast, and to discover that I didn't need or want a replacement, a 'new one'.

A month after my mastectomy, I wrote in my journal, *This is how I am now. And it's all right.* Two months later, I made the decision to be as I am, not to pretend I have two breasts when I have only one. I have never worn my 'new one', my prosthesis, my falsie.

Dr Lin's bucket of cold water was my first real brush with reality. Once I got over the shock I began to understand, as I hadn't quite understood before, how essential it is for our health that reality, and the strong feelings connected with the painful realities, be acknowledged and accepted, not denied. When we are dealing with serious illness the realities of that situation need to be looked at clearly. Acknowledgement and acceptance of the realities offer a way through illness to healing.

Driving home from Leytonstone in tears that day I began to see that I was going to have to turn toward the experience that was in store for me, not away from it; that however painful it was I had to go through it, not round the outskirts of it. This extraordinary thing was happening, and I had to accept it as it was. The rice was boiled.

Out of this growing understanding arose a willingness to face all the facts of my situation, a willingness made manifest on the physical level by the realization that I did not have to conceal my wound behind a false breast. My path through cancer has been eased by not concealing the evidence, by letting my wound be visible.

The changes wrought by breast cancer to our body and our psyche, and to the entire vista of our life and work and relationships and future, are enormous. It can take many months just to assess the scale and scope of the trauma that has taken place, and much longer to come to terms with it. Recovering from surgery is only the beginning.

A woman who has lost a breast knows in her heart that a prosthesis cannot restore her to 'normality', cannot make her 'the same as she was before'. This is not possible. The loss she has suffered cannot be made good by the application of a piece of silicone gel.

The doctors, nurses and support groups who hurry a woman who has just lost her real breast into being fitted with a false one, may do so with the best of intentions, but I am not at all sure it is helpful. At a time when a woman is extremely vulnerable and needs help in facing, accepting and dealing with what has happened to her, and the time and space to do so, it may actually divert her from beginning that essential process, and impede her recovery and healing.

My realization that I didn't need to wear a prosthesis developed gradually over a period of several months. At its heart was acceptance of my changed body and appearance and of having had cancer, with all that this implies; and an instinctive, deep reluctance to assume a disguise, to appear otherwise than as I am. I did not want to hide my 'visible wound'.

Many, perhaps most, women would come to a different decision. But when we have lost a real breast we should be aware that the option not to wear a false one exists, and is valid, and we should allow ourselves time to consider it. Even if we eventually decide to wear a prosthesis, we need, first, to grow used to and be comfortable with how we are now. Then the decision will be a real decision, arrived at after we have had time to absorb the impact of surgery, acknowledge the new reality and begin assessing and accepting the life changes that have taken place.

It should never be done in a hurry, in the wish to 'forget all about it' and 'get back to normal', or in the hope that 'no one will know'. Nor should we do it out of distaste for our changed body, to hide the 'deformity' or to spare others the 'horrible sight'. These are all aspects of denying reality, and we can't afford to do this, for physical and emotional recovery, and true healing, depend on acknowledging and accepting things as they are.

The path of acknowledgement and acceptance leads one gently through the experience of cancer, which is in every way and at every stage a transformative experience. It enables us to digest and assimilate the experience, and integrate it into the new fabric of our life, instead of trying to carry on as if it were just a tiresome blip in the routine, or hadn't happened at all.

It isn't an easy path: there is no such thing as an easy path through cancer. But it is a path that can lead us through the experience to the truths, the rewards, the healing, that are to be found at the heart of it. My great hope for this book is that it will help others to find their way through to their own truths, their own rewards, their own healing.

1   'Prepare to Suffer or to Heal'

When you are told that you have some kind of physical affliction, you can prepare either to suffer or to heal.

This statement, whose source I do not know, leapt out at me from Lidia's bulletin board six months after my diagnosis and surgery, but the attitude it embodies has guided the whole of my journey.

I suppose nearly everyone reacts initially to the shock of a cancer diagnosis as I did, by preparing to suffer. 'Being ill' came as a complete and thoroughly unpleasant surprise to me. I had never been ill, never been in hospital, hardly ever even had a cold. I was always being told how well I looked, and as everyone who knows me exclaimed, I was 'the last person you'd expect to get cancer'. Even when I got cancer, I didn't for a moment feel ill. So it was more than a little difficult for me to accept that I was seriously ill and needed help.

People do want to help, and their help quickens the healing process. But we have to let them give it; we have to ask for help and be able to receive it, and this comes hard for many. At first, it was hard for me. Like many women, perhaps like most women, I have always found it easier to give help and support than to ask for it, or even to acknowledge my own need for it. (Just think how often we say, when asked how we are, 'Oh, I'm fine!' when we aren't really fine; when what we really want to say is 'Well, I'm not so good; I've got a problem and I'd like some help with it.') But at the right moment, I was offered a useful affirmation for people like me: *It's my turn to practise the generosity of receiving.*

It arrived in a letter from someone I hardly know, but to whom I shall always be grateful. I instantly saw the point of it: it opened my eyes to the simple truth that it *is* generous to let people give you the support they want to give, and it opened my heart to all the love and concern that started flowing towards me as soon as people knew that I had cancer.

All this softened me, helped me to begin to accept what had happened and to surrender to it: to accept illness and prepare for healing.

The healing thoughts and prayers of my friends and students created a strong tide of love and support. All through, I was conscious of it buoying me up, carrying me along. Everyone who has felt the healing power of such help will know what I mean. We all wonder, when someone we know is ill or has been bereaved, what we can possibly do or say that might help, and often we give up, thinking there is nothing. But every word, every line, every thought, helps.

Klaus, my husband, has been an unshakeable rock. He has been able simply to be with me through the whole experience, bearing all the pain and the difficulties with me and quietly supporting me in every way. He has always accepted me as I am, and the loss of my left breast made no difference to him. We have been able to share everything with each other from the beginning, when 'everything' was fear and despair. Neither of us has felt that we had to 'be brave' for the other, or that there was anything we couldn't say to each other. This has of course been an enormous help in my efforts to swallow and digest and assimilate the gigantic meal of realities that cancer has fed me. Klaus is the best accepter of reality I know, and I have had his example to follow.

Swami Dharmānanda Saraswati, my teacher, gave me the spiritual guidance I needed to meet the experience and understand its teaching. Alan Stoker, who diagnosed and operated on me at Greenwich District Hospital, was an experienced breast cancer specialist: I was doubly fortunate in that he proved to be a real healer, too. Whenever I saw him in hospital I felt good, and I feel good whenever I see him now. And seven of my students, just completing the initial stage of their teacher training course, took over all my yoga classes without question or hesitation at a week's notice, and continued to teach them for five months, freeing me from anxiety about letting my students down, and from the pressure I would otherwise have felt to hurry back to teaching too soon.

I think I knew I had breast cancer when I left Alan Thompson's surgery that Monday morning. He had been non-committal, but was clearly taking my lump seriously. When he rang me himself a few hours later, to tell me he had made an 'urgent' appointment for Friday of that week with Alan Stoker, I really did know.

That same evening, having spent the afternoon considering what arrangements I would have to make if, as seemed likely, I was going to be out of action for a while, I took three of my students into my confidence.

I heard myself saying the words with disbelief: 'I have a lump in my breast.' I wondered if I was behaving hysterically; I wondered if I was a fraud: the words sounded alarmist, premature, too intense. If the lump turned out to be 'nothing', a cyst, a harmless growth, I was frightening them needlessly, but there was no ignoring my intuition, which told me to speak to them at once. Taking on my classes would challenge them; if they were going to have to do it they would need time to think themselves into it. It was better to risk distressing them unnecessarily now than to wait till I knew for certain and risk the alternative: an emergency situation in which, if I was whisked into hospital quickly, they would have to take over with no time to prepare themselves.

For the past eight years I have taught yoga classes in central London. At the time of my diagnosis I was also teaching a class at a day centre for people with mental health problems, and a group of older people in a sheltered housing block, both in East London. I also run a yoga teacher training course. The three students I spoke to that evening were just completing the first, two-year, stage of the course, and had also been coming to my Monday evening class for three or four years. Shobhna had qualified earlier to teach with the British Wheel of Yoga, and had already been teaching for several years. Annie and Tania, though they had not yet had much experience, were showing themselves to be dedicated and wholehearted, with a true and deep understanding of yoga. I knew, better than they did, that they were quite capable of taking over for me.

I told Shobhna, who arrived early, what was happening – quickly, just the bare facts. She took my hands and said, 'Julie, of course we will look after your classes if you need us to. Don't worry about that.' After the class I talked to the three of them together. I knew it would be a shock to them, but they took it all in, they didn't make a fuss, they just said 'Of course', and showed their love and concern for me in every way. As they were leaving Annie took my hand and said 'It isn't nice, it really isn't nice.' They were reluctant to go; I had to shoo them off. Shobhna said 'We don't want to leave you tonight.'

Over the next few days I spoke to the other students whose help I needed. No questions were asked, no self-doubts voiced, no changes suggested to the arrangements I proposed. They wanted to help me, and when I asked for their help they just said 'Yes, we'll do it, and we'll do it for as long as you need us to do it.' Everything fell into place.

When I look back on this, it seems amazing. And yet, it's not. When you teach yoga – when you teach anything – you accept responsibility for your students. You need to know them, and you need to be able to make accurate assessments of their capacities and their competence. The teacher who gives a student an instruction must know that the student is capable of carrying it out. A student who accepts the instruction of a teacher needs to be able to trust that teacher's competence and judgement, needs to know he or she will not be asked to do anything he or she is not capable of doing. A relationship of trust is established which, as it grows and is repeatedly tested through experience, enables both the student and the teacher to develop and progress.

So when I decided to turn my teaching responsibilities over to my students, I knew they were fully capable of taking on the task. I knew them well, and I knew they could do it. Even more to the point, they trusted me to know it. They may have lacked personal confidence in their ability, but they knew they could trust my judgement.

I had known them all for years, but I had always been 'the teacher', there to answer my students' needs, and I had never had to ask them to answer mine. Now I did, and the immediate result of my opening up to them in this way was an increase of the trust and respect that had already grown between us. In the course of the next five months the whole teacher-training group was to grow closer, and develop stronger bonds. They are still my students and I am still their teacher, but we are now also colleagues, and friends.

Thursday 4 November
I love them and trust them and am terribly fortunate to be able to depend on them now, and I am sure that it will be fine. If this had happened two years ago, or even a year ago, I would have had to suspend the classes at short notice and reconstitute them later on. But now it will be all right, and I know how lucky I am. Clare said 'That's no coincidence, Julie', and of course it isn't – but still, the timing is remarkable. I am grateful, deeply, deeply grateful. To be sure of their love, their respect, their trust, their commitment, their willingness to help. Their love.

Shobhna was to take over the Monday evening class. She was the only one with more than a little teaching experience, and therefore the only one I asked to handle a class on her own. The others were to work in pairs, which I knew would be a good experience for them as well as for their students: Clare and Koye in the Tuesday evening class, and Annie and Tania in the two Thursday evening classes. Other students in the training group were asked to help with setting up before the classes and packing up afterwards.

Caroll would teach the mental health group. She had worked at the day centre and helped me with the class for over a year; she was now a student on the teacher training course. She was working part-time at another centre, and was free on Tuesday mornings to take the class. She knew the clients, and they knew and trusted her. Stella, who had been helping me during the past year with the group of older people, slipped easily into taking charge there.

I was being given the strongest possible support, and I felt it: it was tangible, rock-like; it was like reaching out over an abyss and finding a massive pillar to lean on. I handed my work over to these seven students and they took it on and did it beautifully, until I was ready to take up the reins again.

It was a good experience not only for them, but for the students in the six classes, most of whom had never worked with any teacher besides myself: seeing what a teacher training course could produce inspired more than one of them to apply for the next course. It was a good experience for me, too; so much so that I felt, even at the time, that it made the whole thing worthwhile. I still feel that, and I shall always be grateful to them.

Although I was so fortunate in having people I could hand over to, and although it was a relief to be able to hand over, it was in one respect quite difficult for me to do. From the moment when I hauled my lump into full consciousness and took it to the doctor, I had been protesting: 'How can this be happening? I have too much to do, I love my work too much, I simply don't have the *time* for this.' What I was really saying was 'I can't let go of teaching.' I thought that to let go of teaching, even for a little while, would break my heart.

But letting go of teaching was what I had to do, and doing it, quickly and decisively, taught me an important lesson. It helped me to understand that it is only in letting go that we learn our true strength, that we come into our full power. The Prayer of St Francis of Assisi says:

It is in giving that we receive
It is in pardoning that we are pardoned
It is in dying that we are born to eternal life.

I said that the bond of trust that builds between teacher and student enables the teacher, as well as the student, to develop and grow. If the channels are open and the relationship is nurtured and treasured by both, both will make progress.

In fact, this *must* happen: if it doesn't, if the teacher doesn't change and grow, the student's progress is blocked. It's like Jacob's ladder. You have to keep climbing: if you linger too long on any one rung, you become an obstruction to those following you up. In this unending, universal cycle of spiritual development, the upward movement of your students climbing behind you spurs your own will to progress and thirst for knowledge, and inspires you to keep climbing.

At first, my feelings of trust and confidence in my students, and gratitude to them, were mingled with sadness at having to let go. But my letting go and handing over to them gave them the chance to advance a few rungs up the ladder. For me, it created a space in which I could forget about my work for several months and let go of all the accretions that accumulate when one has been teaching for a long time without a break. When I returned the following April it was with a freshness and an ease, and a deeper commitment and conviction arising out of all that had happened to me.

On Saturday 6 November the teacher training group met. I had spoken individually to the students who were to take over for me, but now I addressed the whole group of fourteen. By now things were clearer. The day before, Alan Stoker had examined me, done a needle biopsy on my lump and arranged for a mammogram. He had been going to leave it at that, not wanting to commit himself to a view or discuss it further until the following Friday when he had the results of the tests and could make his diagnosis. But I asked him outright what he thought. I said I needed to know, because if I was going have to arrange for my classes to be taken over, I needed time to do it.

He answered: 'I'm suspicious of this one. I'm 90 per cent certain you'll need surgery.'

That was, as far as I was concerned, the moment of my diagnosis, unofficial though it was. (It was, naturally, a moment of the deepest shock: when I got off the examination table I could hardly stand.) So when I talked to the teacher training group the following day, I was all but certain that the scenario I was describing was the one that was going to unfold, and that they were really going to have to do what I was asking of them. We sat in a circle, late in the afternoon, and I spoke. I told them what was happening, what Alan Stoker had said, what was likely to happen, and what I wanted them to do. I handed over to them.

Early the next morning, at about 4am, unable to sleep, I was sitting on the floor in my room, crying, praying for help. I was beginning to take in the full import of what was happening to me, beginning to realize that there was no way I was going to get through this on my own strength, without help. At a point during that long night, something happened. Disbelief in my misfortune, anger at my fate, dissolved and were transformed into acceptance. Grim determination to 'beat this thing' and survive turned to surrender, terror to comprehension. It was like the drawing-out of some deeply imbedded malevolent sting. As I wept, as I prayed, I suddenly saw the group before me, saw us all, sitting in a perfect circle, and I saw all their faces. I thought I had handed over to them earlier that day, but it was in that moment that I truly let go.

A few days later, I wrote:

> **Thursday 11 November**
> 'Handing over.' I've never used the phrase as Pam does, but I realized then that that's what I'd done. Handed over. I'd spoken to the group about how difficult it was for me to let go of teaching, but now that I'd done it it no longer seemed difficult. I saw the circle in front of me, the group all sitting together, and saw their faces, and thought, yes. I have handed over to God/over to them. And that it was the same thing.

A wave of release, of relief, trust, gratitude, love, joy, swept over me, so profound it stopped my tears. Everything grew quiet. The moment was a turning point, *the* turning point. In that moment, I let go of suffering, turned around, and let my healing begin.

I had feared – consciously – that having to let go of teaching would break my heart. It didn't. I had believed – not consciously – that my teaching was what defined me, described me, gave me my *raison d'être;* that without it I would cease to be myself. That didn't happen. I let go, and I was still there. In handing my teaching over to the students whom I trusted, just as in handing over the entire experience and its outcome to God, I was surrendering, preparing for healing.

The next day, Sunday, I drove up to Harlow to see Swamiji. In the ten years I have known her she has guided me, and everything she has foreseen for me has come to pass. For example, she told me not long after we met that I was capable of training teachers and that was what

I would be doing eventually. As I had only just begun training to teach, and was still petrified at the mere thought of standing in front of a class, I had to take that on trust. Six years later it happened.

In a conversation with her only a few months before I discovered that I had breast cancer, she said that I would write books containing the deeper insight I was soon to develop. Again I took it on trust, having no idea that the greatest learning experience of my life lay immediately ahead.

Swami Dharmānanda Saraswati is a great spiritual teacher, with extraordinary powers of vision and understanding. I wanted her to see me, I wanted her to look at me, I wanted her to tell me I would 'be all right'. And she did. 'You will be all right,' she said. 'You'll live, because you haven't finished the work you were put here to do.' She gave me spiritual healing, and we talked. When I left her I felt secure and strong, steady and confident, ready to face whatever lay ahead. When she told me I would be all right I believed her, as I always have. Merging with the surrender of the night before, her words calmed and strengthened and softened me. It was a great gift that she gave me.

I shared it with Klaus when I got home, and with all my students the following week. It felt right to speak to them openly about what was happening to me, not to be secretive. Voicing the truth aloud to them helped me to reach out for the support I needed; it helped to make what was happening real.

I was also acutely conscious of the effect my trouble would have on my students. Cancer is a shock to everyone who is close to us. I knew there was no way I could protect them from that shock; I could only help them deal with it by being clear and truthful. People can usually handle the truth, once they know it.

In any case, the effort it would have taken to hide the truth, even if I had wanted to keep it to myself, would have been more than I could cope with. It was easier for me, as well as better for the students, to be honest with them. From the letters I received, and the comments that were made afterwards, I know that my candour helped others to handle their concern for me – and in some cases their concerns about themselves.

So when I taught my classes on Monday and Tuesday and Thursday, I finished by bringing each group of students into a circle to tell them what was happening to me and about the arrangements I had made. I told them what a staunch support yoga was proving to be, and how it was helping me through these testing days and nights. This was something I could give them. Here I was, in the midst of grave crisis, manifesting the truth of all I had been teaching them for years. I told them what Swamiji had said, told them that I believed it, because she had always been right about me, and that they could believe it too.

The diagnosis still hadn't been made, but I was regarding Alan Stoker's '90 per cent certainty' as being as good as certain. It was easier for me to do this, and plan the immediate future on that basis, than to cling to the 10 per cent hope that remained. There was still the chance of a miracle, and it would be great if it happened, but I wasn't going to count on it.

As it turned out, owing to a discrepancy in the test results, the certainty didn't reach 100 per cent until I entered hospital for surgery.

> **Friday 12 November**
> Saw Alan Stoker. The results were inconclusive. The mammogram showed a large carcinoma, but the cytology didn't support it. There were some cancer cells, but not enough to confirm a positive diagnosis. However, he is still '90 per cent sure' it is malignant. (Klaus said later 'It might at least have gone up to 95 per cent by now!') There is a swelling of a gland in the armpit.
>
> He outlined the two ways of treating it: lumpectomy including axillary clearance (removal of the lymph nodes), which would have to be followed by six weeks of radiotherapy, or mastectomy including removal of the lymph nodes, with no radiotherapy. The lump is 3 $\frac{1}{2}$ centimetres, which is beyond the size for which he would want to consider conservative surgery, though he does a great deal of that. If the new test proves conclusive, which he is pretty certain it will (he then did another biopsy, this time with a hollow needle that extracted a thin sliver of tissue, not just fluid: it hurt more!) he would recommend a mastectomy. With the lumpectomy there is always the danger of a local recurrence, which wouldn't be the end of the world and could be dealt with, but a mastectomy might then be necessary anyway. Then he looked at me sharply and said, 'It really depends on how you feel about a mastectomy.'
>
> I said, 'I want my life, and I want to do whatever is going to give me the best chance of keeping it. I have my husband, and I have work to do, and I want to live. A mastectomy wouldn't be the end of the world, and if that's how it has to be, I'll have a mastectomy.'

I think this is what I really do feel. Klaus and I talked about it while Alan Stoker was out of the room. He said, 'Are you sure?' and I said yes: I wanted to get it over with, with the least possible chance of recurrence. I didn't want to have the worry of that, and I didn't want to go through all this upheaval again. And I don't. I want to do what will give me the best chance of a complete recovery and the least chance of a recurrence. So I do feel inclined to accept the mastectomy. It will be an inconvenient nuisance to have to wear a bra with the prosthesis, but I'll just have to put up with that. Not having to have radiotherapy is a plus, too. He said it would take me a month to recover from the surgery, and they don't start radiation till then.

Something has really shifted. Comparing how I feel now with how I felt last Friday, there is a real difference. I've absorbed the shock of knowing I have cancer, and have gone through a great deal of anticipatory grief and fear. At some point during the week I accepted. I surrendered. I let go. I realized that a transformation was occurring, that this is what this experience is for, and I welcomed it. Since then, and especially since seeing Swamiji, although there have been bad moments, I have not felt *afraid*.

And now what I feel – I think – is 'Right, that's that, we know, now let's get on with it.' I actually feel quite all right – no fear-butterflies or grief-tuggings. I know what they feel like now, and I haven't got them just now. They may come again, and I'll accept them ('Hello, fear,' as Lidia says). I know what shock feels like now, and I haven't got that either. My breast is a bit sore from the needling, that's all.

I like Alan Stoker. He talked to us. He was clear and concise and matter-of-fact, he let me ask questions and answered them fully. He seems professional, competent, considerate. His hands are good. We were sizing each other up all the time, very observantly. He has keen eyes. When I asked him if he would do the operation, he said, 'Yes I will.' When I asked him not to cut my muscle he said he wouldn't. I think I'm in good hands there. But – I'm in God's hands, so of course I'm in good hands.

When Alan Stoker returned to the room I told him I had decided, and he said 'I can do it for you next Friday.' I agreed. I had made the decision and I was ready: I felt I didn't need more time, and there was no point in delaying. If it was going to happen, I wanted to get on with it.

Not everyone would want to decide so quickly. Remember, though, that I had been told a week earlier what the diagnosis was more than likely to be, and I had spent that week coming to terms with it. As it happened, that was all the time I needed, but many women facing the prospect of mastectomy might need more time to absorb the shock and consider the options. That time should be taken. Barring unusual circumstances, a few weeks will make no difference to the outcome. But it may well make a difference to our feelings about mastectomy surgery if we have taken part in the decision and not had it imposed upon us. It may also affect how we cope afterwards with the inevitable physical and emotional pain.

The following Thursday, at about 4pm, after I had settled into the bed we had waited for nearly all day, Klaus left me at the hospital. I had thought I might droop and pine once I was alone, but I didn't. Being in hospital was too new and interesting. I felt strong and confident, prepared for what was coming, and indestructible.

Shock has a stimulating, galvanizing effect on mind and body: the adrenal glands start pumping an extra supply of adrenaline into the bloodstream to meet the extra stress. Although I didn't realize it at the time, I was definitely 'on a high'. This is clear from my journal entry: the announcement, 'Tomorrow morning I'm having a mastectomy' sounds as if I were anticipating some particularly delightful treat. My admission of 'vacancy', though, gives me away.

Thursday 18 November
I'm in hospital! Tomorrow morning I'm having a mastectomy. I feel all right: calm, a bit vacant. My only fear is that Alan Stoker may for some reason not be able to do the operation. (I had to sign a legally binding consent declaration which included the item: 'I understand that the surgeon who operates on me may not be the doctor who has been looking after me until now' – of course that alarmed me, and Alice the junior house doctor did nothing to reassure me.) But I suppose all will go according to plan, and tomorrow I shall be without my left breast. And then I'll do everything possible to avoid this happening again. I want to live, and I will. Brenda said, 'You just decide you're going to live, and that's that!'

I feel a sense of *completion* – the last two weeks have been so full of learning, so full of grief, fear, love. I handled it well. What did Annie say? 'You've been inspiring, you've inspired us all.' She is just starting to teach the 7.30 class. Annie is truly amazing. So far to come in so short a time. She will be an exceptional teacher.

Koye and Clare will be fine, will work well together. Everyone will enjoy it. Shobhna is marvellous. Tania and Annie will be fine together too. I've no worries. I've let it go.

Funny to be here in bed in a roomful of strangers, five other patients and their visitors, and climb in and out in full view. I feel used to it already. The nurses are nice. And I think Alan Stoker is smashing. As Pat said, 'so kind'. A terrific person, and if he's as good a surgeon as everyone says, I'll be fine.

At home ten days later I caught up with the journal.

Monday 29 November
Although I had been afraid that when Klaus left me I would start feeling forlorn, sad and anxious, I didn't. Thursday evening passed off with visits from Alice and an argument with her about the arnica I had brought in with me to speed healing, and Mr Palin the anaesthetist, who was confidence-inspiring and told me exactly what he was going to do.

I slept well, and Friday morning arrived. I'd been told that I would be prepared for the operation and given the pre-med at 7, so I got up at 6, had a shower and washed my hair. Somehow I hadn't conceived of that possibility; I'd envisaged being wheeled off all grubby and sleepy and feeling not nice. Ann found me a towel and even a hair dryer, and by 6.20 I was clean and fresh and feeling good. I went into the waiting room and did 40 minutes of practice. I decided that as it was going to be my last good stretch for a while, I'd really enjoy it, and I did. I finished with three rounds of Surya Namaskara (the Sun Salutations) facing east, just as the dawn gave way to the rising sun.

Then I went back to bed, was gowned and stockinged, had a sort of shower cap put on and my rings taped to my fingers, and swallowed the three little pre-med pills. Within minutes I was in a state of total relaxation: calm, comfortable, almost euphoric. I must have slept, because the next thing that happened was that my name was called, and I was told I was going to be taken to theatre. I opened my eyes, said 'Fine.' Chinyeri, the Nigerian night nurse who had got me ready, said 'I'll be with you, praying for you.' I fell asleep again on the way to the operating theatre (all of 25 yards).

They woke me up when I got there, and there were Mr Palin and several smiling faces, including Marina's (the medical student who had done a practice interview on me the day before). He said: 'I'm going to inject you now,' and did. I felt the prick, and then heard my name called again. I opened my eyes to see more or less the same smiling faces – and it was all over.

Back in the ward at 11, I asked Sue to ring Klaus, which she eventually did at 12, and he turned up at about 1 (having been told by Alice the previous evening not even to bother ringing until 2! because I'd be 'wiped out'). He looked so glad and relieved to see me awake and all right. And I felt fine: I wouldn't have wanted to run a marathon, but I didn't feel sick or even woozy. I remember my tongue being a bit thick and not forming words properly for the first few minutes – but that was all. Amazing.

Lynne, who had been through her own bout of breast cancer and had had a mastectomy the year before, had been holding my hand on the telephone over the previous fortnight. Our talks had helped me to face surgery more or less calmly. How good, how important, how comforting it is to be able to talk to someone who has had the same experience or a similar one, and can give you practical, factual information as well as friendship and support. Lynne had told me what to expect at every stage, and that had relieved me of a good deal of apprehension. She was very clear and matter-of-fact about it; I had felt like a five-year-old being briefed about everything that was going to happen on the first day of school. By the time I got to the operation, it held no terrors.

Friends came. Kate was first, on the Sunday, two days after the operation. I leapt out of bed to greet her as she put her head round the door; she took a look at my new chest, and said, 'That's all right. Why do women feel they have to wear falsies? What's wrong with having only one breast?' What a tonic!

Alan Stoker came to see me every day, sometimes with his retinue of registrar and house doctors, junior and senior; sometimes on his own. (I didn't realize that this was unusual until much later, when Duncan, one of my students who had just started his own stint as a junior house doctor told me it was unheard of.) He didn't hover in the doorway in a 'just passing by' sort of way; he always came in and sat down to talk. He never said 'How are we today?', and although he had the whole ward round to do and never stayed for very long, his attention while he was with me was completely mine. His presence was comforting, consoling, healing.

On Thursday night, a week after he had removed my breast, I had a sleepless, tearful night of mourning for it. I tried to convey my feelings of shock and loss to him on his visit the following morning. 'I know,' he said. 'It's terrible. One day you're perfectly healthy, and the next this happens. It's terrible. *I know I'm not a woman, but I really do understand.*'

He did, too, and I trusted him completely. Even then I knew it was a blessing to be able to trust like that, and I am quite sure that this trust has been an important factor in my healing.

The results of the tests on the tumour and lymph nodes came back. Alan told me that the tumour had been well differentiated, which was the good news; but that the cancer had spread to two of the nineteen lymph nodes he had removed, which was bad news. I asked him what the prognosis was, and he said, 'Taking it all in all, I'd put it at 60-40 against your having a recurrence.'

I thought: that's not bad, but I can do better. There will be a lot I can do to improve those odds.

After two days on the ward, I had been given a 'side room', where I had privacy and quiet; even my own bathroom and toilet. I was happy there, and although sleeping was difficult and painful then and after I got home (for weeks I couldn't lie on either side, and being on my back all the time was thoroughly uncomfortable) the whole experience was deeply restful. It gave me the same feeling that crossing the Atlantic (on one of the great ocean liners that sadly no longer exist) on my first trip from America to Europe had given me: a sense of being at a remove, out of the world, off the treadmill, sheltered and protected, absolved from all responsibilities. For the first time since that voyage in 1960 I had absolutely nothing to do, and I thoroughly enjoyed it.

The room was soon overflowing with flowers and cards. The current of support and love that had been transporting me from the start turned into a tidal wave. Every morning brought at least a dozen letters, and I realized, as I never had before, how genuinely helpful these things are – even the briefest, simplest message conveys the care and thought of the person who sent it. I had always felt impotent in the face of deep trouble, felt there was nothing that could be said or done to help someone who was seriously ill or bereaved. How wrong I was. Everything, every message, every card, every letter, every phone call helped.

Klaus's painting had ground to a halt; like me, he could think about nothing but what was happening to me. Now he came to see me every day, twice a day, and we spent long, quiet, healing hours together.

One day we discovered that from the window of my room we could see our house, high on the hill above the hospital, about a quarter of a mile away. Tiny, but we knew it by the row of three windows in Klaus's studio in the pitched roof. 'I could wave at you,' Klaus said. We synchronized our watches, and he went home. I watched by my window, and at the agreed time the middle window opened. A big white towel appeared, waving. I stood on a chair and waved a pillowcase back. The hospital is huge, and has hundreds of identical windows; I didn't think he could see me, but I kept waving. We waved and waved, and when the white towel disappeared, I went to the telephone and rang him. 'I saw you,' he said. 'First I saw your red dressing gown and then I saw you waving.' 'I saw you too!' I said. We were thrilled.

That night he fixed a strong lamp on the top step of a ladder, under the window. He left it on all night, every night, and when I woke, which was frequently as I was drinking a lot, I could look out and see it: my beacon light, my home. By 2am all the other house lights had been turned off, and my beacon shone alone. In its glow I felt Klaus's presence and love, and was reminded that there was a world outside the hospital, a life after cancer, after mastectomy. The light shone, beckoning me forward into that life.

Late one densely foggy night, after a cold, snowy day, I woke up and looked out, thinking 'It won't be there, I won't be able to see it.' But it was there, and I did see it. Everything else had disappeared; the world was shrouded, invisible, but my beacon was there, very small and faint, its edges blurry, but *there*, shining all by itself on the hill, through the thick white silence.

When I tell people now that I enjoyed being in hospital, they laugh. But it was a happy time, a time of preparing for healing. I had survived the operation; the tumour was gone. I had begun to accept the loss of my breast and to think I could live comfortably without it. The relief was enormous, and I could feel the current of life running strongly within me.

I thought that was all there was to it, that it was all over. But it was only the tip of the iceberg, and the process of coming to terms with cancer, of digesting the experience, of assimilating it – the process of healing – had only just begun.

2 Detachment and Surrender

God's Grace is always there. You imagine it to be
something somewhere high up in the sky that has to
descend, but really it is inside you, in your heart, and
the moment you surrender the Grace rushes forth,
spouting as from a spring within you.

Ramana Maharshi

I first came to yoga in 1970, in the way that most people in the Western
world do: for exercise. I was interested in all the ways there were of
keeping fit, and when the health club I belonged to suddenly produced
a yoga teacher, I went along out of curiosity to her first lunchtime class.
It only lasted an hour, but by the end of it I was hooked. I was
astonished at how I felt: fully stretched, in a way that I had not
experienced before. My mind felt as though it too had been stretched. I
felt relaxed and cheerful, more in touch with myself, and somehow
opened up. I returned the following week, and have never looked back.

Yoga became increasingly important to me, and for many years now
it has been the mainstay of my life, its nourishing spring. In time, I
began to want to share something of what yoga has given me with
others, and I trained to teach. After teaching for several years, I
became involved in training yoga teachers.

Most people think of yoga as a purely physical activity, and for most it
does indeed start in that way: as something one 'does' once a week or
once a day in order to feel better. But it is a great deal more than that, as
those who continue to practise soon discover. Yoga is an attitude of
mind, a way of being which involves us on all levels: physical, emotional,
mental, and spiritual. Yoga can take us as deep as we want to go, but
those who stay in the shallows experience effects and changes too.

Yoga is a process of spiritual growth. The yoga practices remove the
blockages that trap energy and restrict its flow through our being. They

release energy and enable it to flow freely. When this starts to happen, we can move steadily and surely towards the fulfilment of our potential.

Yoga practice develops the inner strength, steadiness, stability, self-discipline and serenity that enable us to deal skilfully and responsibly with whatever problems and obstacles, whatever tragedies and triumphs life brings us. It teaches us to use all these experiences, whether 'good' or 'bad', 'pleasant' or 'unpleasant', as opportunities for learning and growth. It helps us to live our lives meaningfully, consciously. Through the quiet, attentive self-observation that yoga practice encourages, our awareness expands and our powers of concentration and discernment unfold, and we are led towards inner transformation and spiritual awareness.

I have never underestimated the power of yoga to help us through life. It has never failed me, and since I started teaching I have observed it working in the lives of my students. But during times of crisis that power really declares itself, and in the weeks after I discovered my lump I experienced it as I never had before. As one of my students memorably observed, 'When the chips are down, we see that it really works.'

Yoga is a Sanskrit word, for which the nearest equivalent in English is 'yoking', or 'union'. This can be understood as the uniting of body, mind and spirit and, in the context of practice, as the co-ordination of body, mind and breath. It is the joining of the individual consciousness, the individual self, with the higher consciousness or higher Self; the union of the individual spirit with God. The word yoga is also used to describe the techniques used to attain this goal: it is thus both the process and its outcome, the means and the end.

The *Upanishads* and other classical texts of yoga tell us clearly, in passage after joyous passage, that the Self, or God, is to be found within ourselves, and that it is to be sought in the heart: it dwells there and we don't have to look anywhere else for it. The *Svetasvatara Upanishad* says:

> *The Self is hidden in the hearts of all*
> *As butter lies hidden in cream.*
> *Realize the Self in the depths of meditation –*
> *The Lord of Love, Supreme Reality,*
> *Who is the goal of all knowledge.*

> *He is the inner Self of all,*
> *Hidden like a little flame in the heart.*
> *Only by the stilled mind can he be known.*
> *Those who realize him become immortal.*

In the *Mundaka Upanishad* it says:

> The Lord of Love is the one Self of all. He is detached work, spiritual
> wisdom, and immortality. Realize the Self hidden in the heart, and cut
> asunder the knot of ignorance here and now.

And the *Chandogya Upanishad* tells us:

> A person is what his deep desire is.
> It is our deepest desire in this life that shapes the life to come.
> So let us direct our deepest desires to realize the Self.

Yoga explains that to realize the Self within we need to develop
detachment: detachment from the objects of desire that attract and
involve our senses and draw them outward, from the transitory world of
material possessions and sensory pleasures that obscure the real wealth
that lies within us and divert our attention from it. Yoga also counsels
detachment from the fruits of our work, from our body (and from the
illusion that our body is the whole of us), and from the need to control
the lives of others; and above all, detachment from the illusion that we
are separate from the One Self.

It is often supposed that detachment means lack of emotion,
coldness, harshness; that it dries up our compassion; that it requires us
to stop enjoying life and the things of this world, renounce our
possessions and cease to care about our work and our families and
friends.

Detachment does not mean any of these things. What it means is
that we grow able to experience our emotions and observe them
without getting entangled in them. It means that we can be
compassionate towards the troubles of others without getting involved
with them. It means that although we have possessions we don't get
attached to them: we understand that the things of this world are not
'ours', but only given temporarily into our keeping. It means that we do
our work to the best of our ability, but without attachment to it or its
rewards. It means that we love and cherish our partners, children,
friends without clinging to them, without trying to change or control
them, without making the mistake of thinking we own them.

In learning detachment, we learn to know ourselves better. When
we are able to drop the involvement of our own ego in the troubles of
others (and our tendency to give advice), we can be more genuinely
helpful to them. When we are able to do our work for its own sake,

without concerning ourselves about money and promotion, appreciation and recognition, we can do it better. As the ego becomes subdued it loses its fear of rejection, and then we can open ourselves to others and love more deeply, less selfishly.

The Sanskrit word for detachment is *vairagya*, and it is what enables us to stand back a little from the emotions our experiences give rise to; to observe them without getting entangled in them, to accept them with compassion, to develop discernment and insight with respect to them, and to release them. It is what enabled me to stay steady most of the time during the anxious days of waiting for diagnosis, to hold my balance while my life was being turned inside out by what felt like catastrophe. It helped me too in the longer process of coming to terms with surgery and prognosis. It is helping me now to live fully in the present while acknowledging that the future is unknowable and uncertain, and I know that if my cancer ever recurs, it will help me again.

Getting through cancer is a long process. If we are to get through it at all, and not get 'stuck' in denial, anger, fear or grief, we need to acknowledge the realities of the situation, and accept the strong, often violent emotions that inevitably arise. This is a tall order, because so much that is unfamiliar and frightening happens so quickly, and it's so easy to shut down, to push the feelings away.

If we shrink from feeling our emotions, if we turn away from them when they arise, if we cut them off, they gain strength and trap a tremendous amount of energy. But if we allow them to surface into consciousness and turn towards them; if we acknowledge them, look at them, and own them, they begin to lose their power over us. Once we have let them in, we can let them go. The blocked energy that has been held in them will be released, to be channelled more usefully, more creatively.

No one advocating this process would claim that it is a comfortable one, but the pressure and anxiety that build up inside us when we deny and suppress our emotions are even less comfortable, and ultimately destructive to health and healing. This is true, I think, whatever the circumstances of our life, but it is especially important to understand it when life itself is threatened by serious illness.

The process itself, of allowing our painful emotions into consciousness and looking at them, can be trusted to bring the clarity, steadiness and stability that enable us to examine and master them. Gradually we cease to be ruled by our emotions; gradually we develop detachment and the power of discrimination.

Although I 'knew' this, and had tested it out through many years and kinds of 'ordinary' life experiences, it was put to the ultimate test when I learned that I had cancer. The emotions that arose – shock, anger, terror, grief – were intense, often violent. But there was always a part of me that was able to stand aside and observe them. I found it was possible to feel them, acknowledge them, witness them, without clinging onto them or getting entangled in them.

I found, somewhat to my surprise, that I could have a good cleansing cry for five or ten minutes and then get on with something else: it didn't have to go on for hours and hours. Sometimes we inflate our emotions out of proportion to their importance (we 'gold-plate' them, as Stephen Levine says). We imagine that how we feel now is how we are going to feel forever, and this intensifies the feelings and tightens our hold on them. But strong as they are, they are only emotions, and they won't hang onto us if we don't hang onto them. They will pass if we let them. They will pass more quickly if we understand that they will pass, that they are not the whole of us, and learn to watch them as they come and go instead of getting involved with them.

And we don't necessarily need to 'analyse' everything, or delve into the deeper recesses of our psyche for insights. All that is needed is acceptance and observation of the rising emotions: clarity and insight will follow.

During the first fortnight of November, between the Friday of my visit to my GP and the Friday of my diagnosis, I would wake regularly at 2 or 3am with the full weight of what was happening bearing down upon me. The first time this happened, I realized it could only get worse if I lay there panicking, and I knew what I needed to do. I got up and went into my workroom, switched on the electric heater, sat down on the floor, and started practising breath awareness.

Breath awareness, which has been an integral part of my practice, indeed the foundation of it, for many years, became my support from that first disturbed night onward. I carried on with it during the period before and after the diagnosis. I would surface from sleep in despair, my heart full of fear or grief or both, get up, sit on the floor, cry for a while, and then start to observe my breath. In hospital, and at home again while I was recovering from the operation, this simple, unfailingly effective practice continued to help me maintain the mental poise I needed to look clearly and steadily at all that was happening to me. (If you would like to know more about this simple but extremely helpful technique, you'll find a full explanation and guidance on practising it in Chapter 8.)

Feelings would arise; when they did I let them. Crying was therapeutic, cleansing; it was like letting the steam out of a pressure cooker, and when it was over I returned to watching my breath. In the course of an hour or so this might happen two or three times. By then, having paid attention to whatever emotions had arisen, I was calmer and quieter and was able to go back to bed and sleep for the rest of the night.

At first, I kept asking, as I expect nearly everyone does, 'Why me? How can this be happening to me?' Desperate, angry, I protested at the unfairness of it. I didn't want this to be happening; it couldn't be happening. I had too much to do, I had no time for cancer. It was a monstrous imposition, an absolute negative, a total disaster. Why should this be happening to me now, when everything was going so well, why was I having to face the possibility of early death now, when I had scarcely begun the real, the important work of my life?

After a week of this, the day after my 'unofficial diagnosis', I realized that the question might not be a valid one. It made no difference why it was happening. It just *was* happening. That was how it was, and I had to accept it as it was. In the previous chapter I wrote of the moment when, at 4am on Sunday 6 November, on my knees in a flood of tears, the turning-point came. For the first time in my life I prayed for help. I surrendered to the experience that had been thrown at me, stopped kicking against it, stopped protesting at it, and turned to look cancer and death in the face.

In that moment of surrender I let go of the question, the 'Why?', and having let go of it, immediately got the answer. Instantly, I understood that it was going to be a complete transformation, a healing transformation, and that it was necessary for my future life and growth and all that I hope to do and to be that I undergo it. And I knew that I could welcome it, knowing I was in God's hands.

Occasionally there is an experience in one's life that one looks back upon, knowing that it was important, that it was a turning point; an experience of which it seems that everything that has happened before it has led up to it, and everything that has happened subsequently has led on from it. More rarely, one knows as it as it is happening that it is one of those. I felt then, and have never since doubted, that that moment of surrender and acceptance was the critical moment, the pivot on which my life would turn, the instant in which my whole being accepted what was happening and welcomed it, with complete trust, as transformation. In that moment I knew that I could and would go through it and live.

That night, I talked to God. I hadn't ever done that before. At first, all that came out was a host of angry 'Why me's?', a litany of complaint and despair. And then suddenly I said – where did the words come from? – 'All right. I can't deal with this on my own, I'm not strong enough for it, and I'm handing it over to you. It is going to happen, and I am going to go through it, and it is going to change me. Let it happen. I'm ready for it now. I accept it. And I even look forward to it. I look forward to seeing whatever it makes of me, whatever I become through it, whatever I turn out to be on the other side of it.'

The question had changed; it had become not 'Why?' but 'How?' How am I going to use this experience?

A few days later, I wrote in my journal:

Thursday 11 November
So much has happened this week. I'll never be able to get it all down, and certainly not in the order it has all happened. At teacher training on Saturday I spoke to the group and told them the arrangements I had in mind for the classes. Everyone simply listened, and said 'Yes, of course'. The strength of the group supported me through it, and although I had been a little wobbly once or twice during the day, I was steady then. Afterwards no one crowded me; one by one they came up and spoke to me and let me know how they felt.

That night, when I couldn't sleep, I went to my room and sat. This was at about 4am. I cried violently – the crying is incredible. I can't remember having ever cried like this, except in New York ten years ago after my father died. Grief crying, from the depths. And I prayed. For the first time in my life, I was able to pray. Lord, please let me live. I want to complete the work you sent me here to do. And also for Klaus, Lord, for my darling. Please let me live. Because when his time comes I want to be with him and see him through. Please let me live. And then I surrendered, and put myself in God's hands.

I felt my heart opening, opening and loosening. It felt as though a knot, a literal, real knot, had been untied somewhere deep inside me. Then came an incredible sensation of peace, of stillness, and I said 'Thank you,' and rested.

In the *Mundaka Upanishad* there is a passage that says:

When that Self, which is both cause and effect, is realized, the knot of the heart gets untied, all doubts become resolved, and all one's actions become diminished.

As I felt my own knot unravelling, I knew that 'my own strength', which I had always been able to rely on, had even prided myself on, wasn't going to be enough to get me through, but that there was a greater strength behind me that was, and would. Even so, I was unprepared for how much I would be given when I asked. From that moment, everything changed. What I needed was given instantly, a great weight was lifted, and the desperate sense of struggle dissolved and vanished.

The following week I received a letter from Shraddha (the name is Sanskrit, and it means 'faith'), a wonderful letter which I treasure. 'When you know you need help,' she said, 'you must ask for it, *really* ask. Ask and you will receive, knock and the door will be opened.' A few days earlier, I would have thought 'That's right: I understand this, I know this is true.' But then, I would have understood only the words. Now, I really did understand it.

Now, I knew that I would be given the strength to deal with whatever happened. I had asked, and been answered. I had knocked, and the door had opened. I had touched some source deep inside myself. The passage from the *Mundaka Upanishad* had become truth for me; it had happened exactly as described: the knot of my heart got untied, all my doubts became resolved, and all my actions became diminished.

Knowing this, knowing that I couldn't do all the work myself, and that I didn't have to, was an immense relief. Since then it has seemed to me that whatever is being done, God is doing it, and I am just helping. That trust has underpinned the entire journey, and has helped me to accept things as they are.

Months later I was given a copy of an unpublished article about death and dying by Jean Klein, called 'The Great Forgetting'. He says:

> It is only in accepting, in welcoming, that all the elements of a situation
> can be clearly seen. When we live in accepting illness has no hold,
> no substance, and we have the greatest possibility of getting better. [1]

How perfectly that affirmed what I had discovered for myself.

When, as has happened once or twice, someone expresses surprise that 'With all your yoga, how could you possibly get cancer?', I simply say that yoga is an attitude of mind, an all-embracing philosophy and way of living, not an exercise system, and that it is yoga that has enabled me not only to 'get through' the experience, but to use it, to turn it into something good.

It has certainly been the most difficult and testing experience of my life, but if I was offered the chance to go back in time and avoid it, I would refuse. Cancer has changed me. The changes have enriched my life and my teaching and will be important in all my work from now on.

Having cancer, recovering from cancer, learning to live with cancer, has given me knowledge and insight that I did not have before, and could not have gained in any other way. It has shown me how precious each moment of life is; has made me realize that nothing in life can be taken for granted, and so has brought life into sharper focus. It has taught me acceptance and surrender. Paradoxically, perhaps, it has also given me confidence, quickened my power to act and speak surely and decisively. It has given me more to offer in my teaching, and through my writing. It has taught me that there is nothing to be afraid of. It has given me a greater measure of peace.

The power behind you is greater than the task in front of you.

For several years, this has been a touchstone for me: one of those rocks we hold onto whenever the going is rough. It has strengthened and heartened me whenever I have had to face a challenge, and now I know, better than before, how deep its truth lies. When we really ask for help, the strength and energy and faith we need are given to us. In that moment of letting go, in surrendering the experience to God, I finally understood that it isn't 'our' strength, 'our' energy that brings us through; it is God's strength, God's energy. Instantly, I accepted whatever was to come, and my panic and shock receded. Knowing, now, where my strength comes from, knowing it isn't 'mine', has made me stronger than before, but it's the quieter, surer strength of acceptance and surrender, rather than the combative strength of struggle and battle.

This knowledge, this trust, doesn't absolve us from our personal responsibility, or from our role in the healing process. Our job is to help, and we have to give ourselves to it wholeheartedly; we have to *use* the gifts, the help, and the strength we are given. It's a joint effort, delightfully illustrated in the story about the man of faith who, marooned on a rooftop in a rising flood, knew that God would save him. A rowboat came by, but he waved it away, saying 'God will save me.' A helicopter flew over the house, but he refused to get into it, saying 'God will save me.' So he drowned, and the first thing he asked God when he got to Heaven was 'Why didn't you save me?' And God answered, 'I did try to save you. I sent you the rowboat, and I sent you the helicopter, but you wouldn't use them.'

Yoga philosophy teaches that the world is there for us to experience, and that through our experience we gain knowledge and eventually liberation from the bonds of ignorance that obscure our true nature and prevent our knowing who we really are. When we are given a truly testing experience, one that shakes our foundations, we naturally wish at first that we hadn't. But we have, like it or not; it's ours to learn from, and it's the most painful experiences that have the most to teach us. And perhaps we don't need to ask 'why' we have been given this particular experience, why this apparent obstacle has been put in our path. We may never know why, and it doesn't really matter. The real question must be: What are we going to do with the experience? All that matters is how we use it.

Someone remarked recently: 'I suppose the worst thing about having cancer is that you can't trust your body any more.' It's true that we don't know what may happen. But then we never did know. And it's possible to learn to live comfortably with 'don't know'. For me, the loss of trust on the physical plane has been abundantly repaid by the increase of trust on every other level, and in every aspect of my life.

The detachment developed through yoga helped me in another way. Through yoga I have come to know that we are not just our bodies; that the body is only a vehicle for the passage through life, a temporary dwelling for the spirit. And when my body was threatened with what is generally regarded as a terrible mutilation, it turned out that this was a real knowing, not just a bit of intellectual posturing. When Alan Stoker recommended a mastectomy and left the decision to me, I didn't hesitate: I knew my left breast was dispensable, a part of my body I could live without. At my age – 58 – it was a non-functional gland; I didn't need it, and it struck me that the loss of it would be a good deal less inconvenient than the loss of a finger or a toe. It remained to be seen whether I would continue to feel like this after it was gone, but after some initial sadness, and some work on reclaiming the wounded area, I did, and it has been easy to accept my body as it now is, knowing that I haven't been in any way diminished.

I know, of course, that a younger woman's feelings might be very different, especially if chemotherapy or removal of her ovaries puts her into early menopause. I can only say how it was for me. But I was heartened at the response of a young woman who had breast cancer at the age of 29. After Heather had read the book in manuscript we discussed this aspect of it, and I asked if my experience had been at all relevant for her. She said: 'Of course there are differences in circumstances and in our reactions to them, but the lesson is the same.'

It was harder, and took longer, to learn to live with the loss of certainty about the future. I had always assumed that my strong constitution and untroubled health would last me through life without any major upheavals (I know that was a bit unrealistic!). Did I think I was immortal? Perhaps not, but I certainly took my health and strength and resilience for granted, thought myself invulnerable to common ills, and felt assured of a long and – I hoped – useful life. I confidently expected to trundle on till 87 or thereabouts, with all my faculties intact. Of course I may still get to 87, with my faculties if not my body intact, but that no longer seems a certainty. I realize now that it was a false certainty, but the loss of it was painful, and coming to terms with it took time.

It was painful, but there is another side to it. That false certainty, that self-reliance, have been replaced with something new: a more intense joy in being alive, a clearer sense of what is and isn't important, a greater pleasure in laughter, a strengthening of the bonds with others, a deeper trust in myself and in others, and in the love of my husband and my friends and in mine for them, trust in the power of love to help and heal, an understanding of where my strength comes from. These are blessings, and I am grateful for them.

But the greatest blessing of all, the one from which all the others flow, is the acceptance I have come to, the acceptance of reality, including the reality of mortality, of death. The thing is as it is. I need waste no energy pretending it is otherwise. There are times, of course, when this knowledge is difficult to bear. There may be times to come when it will be very difficult to bear. But all in all, acceptance gives me peace. It frees me to be wholly myself, to live fully now.

A cancer diagnosis is not necessarily a death sentence. Nevertheless, once you have had cancer, the reality of death is never very far away. This is what cancer sufferers who get stuck in denial are denying. Denial arises out of fear and is all too understandable. But cancer gives us a tremendous opportunity, the opportunity to acknowledge death and accept it before it comes to us. It opens a window onto a deeper truth. Looking through the window now helps prepare us for that eventual reality. And while we are still here, it thrusts us into fuller, richer, more conscious life.

3   'Death is Simply a Fact of Life'

> Men are disturbed not by things, but by the views
> which they take of things. Thus death is nothing terrible,
> but the terror consists in our notion of death.
>
> Epictetus

In the second chapter of the *Bhagavad Gita*, Lord Krishna says to Arjuna:

Thy tears are for those beyond tears; and are thy words words of wisdom? The wise grieve not for those who live; and they grieve not for those who die – for life and death shall pass away. (II:11)

For all things born in truth must die, and out of death in truth comes life. Face to face with what must be, cease thou from sorrow. (II:27)

Invisible before birth are all beings and after death invisible again. They are seen between two unseens. Why in this truth find sorrow? (II:28)

Why indeed in this truth find sorrow? But we do. I had studied and, I thought, comprehended the teachings of the *Bhagavad Gita* and the *Upanishads* and other texts, and I really thought I wasn't afraid of dying, but when I knew I had cancer I found out I was – or at least I found myself clinging fiercely to life and sorrowing deeply at the prospect of leaving.

But as time passed and the experience unfolded, this desperate clinging abated. My grip loosened. I still hope with all my heart to live a long time, but I'm not clinging quite so hard, now. This letting go, this acceptance of the uncertainty of life and the inevitability of death, has revealed to me something that I thought I knew, but did not really know, in the days of false certainty.

Life in this body does not go on forever, but Life itself goes on. The Self within each of us is eternal; it does not, cannot die. I thought I knew this before – but perhaps I only believed it. There is knowing, and knowing.

At first, no protective barriers arose to shield me from the implications of cancer, and I instantly took in the possibility that I might die. It wasn't that I thought I had been 'given a death sentence'; I knew that cancer is not necessarily fatal, that many people make full recoveries and live out a normal life span without recurrence. It was simply a total, vivid, shocking awareness of the possibility. For the first time in my life I had come face to face with my death.

For the first two weeks I was overwhelmed. Great waves of grief and terror kept washing over me at the prospect of dying and leaving Klaus, dying before I had completed my work in life. Standing, weeping, in the kitchen in Klaus's arms after our first meeting with Alan Stoker, I spoke my fear. I said, 'I might die.' Astonished, he countered, 'You're not going to *die* of this.' 'People do,' I said.

During this time I was doing something important, though I didn't realize it till much later. I was looking over the edge of a precipice at the possibility of my death. I made myself do it: I trained my eye on it and kept it steady there. But then, for a while, I averted my gaze. After the diagnosis and the decision for mastectomy had been made, I shifted gears and focused all my attention on getting rid of the tumour, cleansing it out of my body, overcoming the threat to my life. In the week between diagnosis and surgery, and for several weeks afterwards, I simply refused to consider death, or the possibility of cancer recurring. In hospital, on a wave of triumph, euphoric at having survived surgery, I gathered my energies and directed them towards getting better. Forging ahead, ignoring everything else, I concentrated on my body, and it recovered quickly.

Death was not part of my equation. A friend sent me a copy of Bernie Siegel's *Love, Medicine and Miracles*; reading it, I answered an immediate, resounding 'Yes' to his key question: 'Do you want to live to be a hundred?' I did want to. Unequivocally. No reservations, no doubts. Recovering from cancer begins, he says, with a decision to live, and the decision has to be made by every cell in one's body. I felt certain that that decision had been made by every one of my cells and that I would recover, that I would be healed, and that I would live, because I wanted to.

I still want to. But I understand now that healing is not about curing the body or about outwitting death. It's about living, living fully. It's about accepting and welcoming all that life holds for us, including dying. We may strive our utmost, with all our strength, motivation and determination to cure the body, but in the end, the body is going to die. A vital part of healing is letting this truth in, understanding that we can heal towards dying, heal into death. Accepting this doesn't mean that we've given up, or become morbid or lost hope. It means that we have embraced reality.

In *The Tibetan Book of Living and Dying*, Sogyal Rinpoche says:

> When we accept death, transform our attitude toward life, and discover
> the fundamental connection between life and death, a dramatic possibility
> for healing can occur. [2]

Death is not failure; it is simply, as Sogyal Rinpoche says, 'a fact of life'. We are all going to die, and whether it happens tomorrow or next year or in forty years, or at any time in between, is not the point. Nobody lives forever; none of us is given 500 years. This is how it is. What matters is what we do with the years, the days, the moments, we are given, how we use our life experiences, and how we prepare ourselves for dying.

During the six weeks it took my body to recover, I totally erased the thought of death from my mind. But once that relatively short and uncomplicated stage was over, it began to creep back in. Again it was terrifying – though not quite as terrifying as it had been at the beginning.

For the first few days of creeping fear, I increased my difficulty by clinging to the notion that I wasn't afraid. I really did think I wasn't. I thought I had done all the confronting, all the working out I needed to do. I thought I had 'dealt with everything' in that momentous three weeks before going into hospital. Of course I hadn't. To put myself further off the track, I had also taken it into my head that fear was a killer, the most 'negative' (ie 'bad') emotion one could have, that being afraid was an adverse sign, an immune system depressor, an ominous indication that one's resolve, one's will, one's determination to live, might be weakening.

So I had decided that I wasn't going to be afraid.

But I *was* afraid, and denying it was turning the screw of fear tighter and tighter inside me. This actually showed itself physically. After several days of resolutely pushing my rising fears back down, I developed an intense, knife-like pain in the region of my left shoulder blade. It went away as soon as I stopped trying to fool myself and acknowledged that I had entered a new stage, that there was more to do.

It was a long process. During the first year, I gradually learned what to do when a fear surfaced. I simply looked at it, recognized it, and waited for it to pass, which it always did. While it was there, I lived with it. I did not find this too difficult as long as I didn't pretend it wasn't there. It's the energy and effort it takes to hold fear down that make it so hard, so exhausting, to cope with.

Writing my journal helped me make the transition from physical recovery to the next stage: looking at fear and letting it in.

I had started the journal on 4 November in response to my deep certainty that this was what I needed to do, and it had been greatly helpful from the outset; gradually I realized how essential to the healing process it was going to be.

Writing a journal helps us to get in touch with our buried feelings. It gives us a means of unearthing them, examining them, acknowledging them, and – eventually – letting go of them.

My journal has become part of my life; it is necessary to me. As time goes on I use it more and more for life-issues that are not related to cancer. But at that time, starting from about six weeks after the surgery when my fears started to rise, it was about fear: fear of recurrence, fear of death.

Through journal-keeping I was able to work through my fears. But at first, I wrote about them only to deny them.

Monday 27 December
Erwin rang this evening from Melbourne. He sounded so pleased to hear me sounding cheerful. Then he asked me if everything was 'all right', if the pathology had shown that everything was all right. And I had to explain about the affected nodes, and the prognosis. It could recur, I said: once you've had cancer there is always that possibility. *But it isn't going to.* As I said the words, with emphasis, I could hear them sounding brave and a little hollow to Erwin, and that surprised me. And shook me a little. Maybe I ought to be feeling afraid? But no. It would be no help. And I'm not afraid. I do feel well, and I know I am being looked after, and I know there will be no more cancer.

And yet, everything has changed. I've entered a different dimension, my outlook has altered. I know now that I can die. And that it could be sooner than I thought. I might not have another thirty years, or even twenty. I could die in my sixties.

This is a fact. As I write this, I know I have admitted the possibility. It has entered my consciousness and made everything different. Life is precious, being with Klaus is precious, every moment is precious. I don't think I will die soon – but I have without a doubt acknowledged the possibility.

Not long afterwards I read something that rocked me, and this time I had to admit it.

Tuesday 4 January
Reading, in the book Christine lent me, *Your Cancer, Your Life*, about the 'seedlings', the stray cancer cells that may lurk in the blood and take anything from one to twenty years to show up in some organ or in the bone or brain, did frighten me. But I knew all about that before: why am I frightened now? Because my mind is allowing the fear to break in. And now I have to deal with it. I blurted it out to Klaus today, saying 'What if it comes back?' and 'It's so insidious: it can lurk there in the blood and then pop up in two years or ten years in the liver or lungs or bones.' He thought about it for a few moments, and then said 'It could do that even if you hadn't had it now: it could pop up in two years or ten years, just like it popped up now. So what's the difference?' My immediate reaction was that having already had cancer made it different, and he admitted that it probably increased the chances. But it is an interesting way of looking at it. That one never knows what's around the next corner.

Anyway, it all just seems enormous, incredible, unbelievable. The very choice of those words is the clue: I have not really taken it in yet. I keep saying 'I need time, a lot of time, just to absorb.' Perhaps I hadn't, haven't, yet fully realized what there is to absorb.

I think now that in the days and weeks immediately following the operation I was being carried forward on the crest of a wave: of will, of relief, of adrenaline, of determination to 'be all right'. As I admitted to Tania, I made light of the pain. The truth is that I hardly let myself acknowledge even the physical pain, which was considerable. This has become more and more apparent as it eases off. Every day has brought an improvement: the more the pain recedes, the less of it there is – and it is now six whole weeks, six weeks of 'improving' – the more I realize how much of it there was. When I think of how I looked, black and blue all over my left shoulder, chest and side, and how I couldn't turn over, couldn't tolerate any pressure on either side – when I remember all that, I can see how much pain there was, how much room for 'improvement' there was. Yet right after the operation I remember thinking, and assuring everyone, that I wasn't in much pain.

Yes, there was considerable pain. But I made light of it. And perhaps I also made light of, or did not even take in, the rest of the pain, the emotional pain. But there is a lot of that, too. And I need time to take it in. This is just the beginning.

T (who gave me acupuncture while N, the practitioner of Traditional Chinese Medicine I was seeing, was away) said 'You don't seem disturbed.' I said that wasn't quite true, that there had been a lot of emotion, and that I needed to cry a lot and did. But I think she was saying, 'You don't look disturbed, but you should be, and it's not natural that you aren't.' Just as Mr Stoker and his team were perplexed by my calmness and good spirits in hospital. I remember sensing the same reaction from N, when I said I wasn't afraid. He smiled quizzically, not wanting to challenge me, but as if to say 'But you should be, it would be realistic to be, it would be surprising if you weren't – and in fact, I don't believe you.'

So what is all this telling me? To be clear, to be truthful, to get on with letting go, with feeling, experiencing, clearing. And stop trying so hard to make everyone think I'm 'all right'. I didn't want to tug on people for sympathy, I didn't want anyone to think I 'couldn't cope', wasn't strong, wasn't positive.

But why do I have to do that? Why do I have to make people think I'm all right? Why am I afraid that people might think I can't cope? What's wrong with not being all right after a cancer operation? What would be wrong with not coping for a bit? I don't have to do this. And I'd better try to stop it.

As soon as I could drive, I went up to Harlow to see Swamiji. We had spoken frequently by telephone, but I needed to see her now; I wanted her guidance on a number of things, and fear was at the top of the list.

Thursday 6 January
I can say anything to her, and was frank about my fears. And saw, while we spoke, that I have been making things extra hard for myself by fastening onto my 'I'm all right, I'm not afraid'

hitching post. I wasn't afraid then because I was coping with my physical recovery. Now that that is almost complete, my consciousness knows it can start coping with the emotions, the fears, and that's beginning to happen. By going on with the 'I'm not afraid' stance once that initial stage was past, I was making it doubly difficult.

I realized in talking to Swamiji that I must now simply go along with the process, take it as it comes, and acknowledge whatever feelings come up. I knew all this, and shouldn't have needed to prove it to myself, but it seems I did. If only I can 'just be', and not get attached to what I was, or what I felt, or how I was, yesterday or last week. The post-operative effort of will, soaring upwards and onwards, is over. My body is better, or nearly so. Now starts the next stage. It is, as I thought, a long, slow process of absorbing. If I hang onto the protective barriers, or to whatever I was feeling in a previous stage, I won't be able to 'absorb' anything through the hard surface.

She said, 'You're clear *now*. If you get a recurrence in however many years, you'll deal with it *then*.' We agreed that it was natural and realistic to be frightened, but that I shouldn't let it rule me.

She pointed out that if I had had to cope with all the emotional things earlier on, it would have made the process of physical recovery much harder and slower. So the protective barrier was part of the healing process.

I was beginning to let things in, beginning to let the thought of death re-surface. A week later an unsettling conversation with a friend gave me a shove in the right direction.

Thursday 13 January
I am thrilled about my progress. I have all the arm movement back and almost all the stretch. When I do the elongating stretches now, I can feel the stretch on my left side, and it's a wonderful feeling. On the floor, my elbow touches with the arm much more nearly straight than a week ago. I can almost do a good chest expansion, though that still pulls hard across the front. Zena (my physiotherapist) has been a great help: I'm sure it would have been a much longer job without her. Every day there is noticeable improvement, especially after I have been to her. She moves me further than I can move by myself, and then

when she's done it I'm there, and can work from there. There have been no setbacks.

I've begun to feel little stirrings, little inner flickers, of wanting to teach. I'm not ready yet for the regular classes, but the experience of teaching on Saturday (at the teacher training group) was good. I started the day off, just waited to hear my voice and what I would say, and it sounded different. Sue said 'Your voice sounded younger, and lighter.' And Sophie said 'It was wonderful to hear your voice: it was like coming home.' After that I started to feel eager and happy about the prospect of teaching again. And I know now that I'll know when it's time, when I'm ready.

Right now I think I'm still too preoccupied with myself to give it my best, to give it all of myself. I felt, at Harvey Nichols, when I got so worked up about not finding the bra there, that I really am on a short fuse these days – everything very close to the surface, all right when nothing happens to upset me, but easily tipped off balance when something does. And this morning, I was completely thrown by my conversation with Pat. I need to get back on a more even keel before taking on the regular commitment again. This was what happened with Pat:

'How old are you?
'58.'
'Well you've had a good innings, you've had your life with Klaus, and if you get another 5 or 10 years that will be pretty good going.'
'But I'm not looking for 5 or 10 years, I want 30 years.
'Everyone feels that. I haven't read Don Quixote yet.'
'That's not the same thing. I have work to do, and I want the time to do it!'
'You don't want to live to 88, do you?'
'Yes I do, or at least 83.'
'You're not going to be teaching yoga at 83?'
'Yes, in one way or another.'
'All right – but if something happens in five years, don't be angry. You never know what's round the corner.'
'I will be angry. I'll be very angry.'
'No you won't.'
'Yes I will, certainly at first.'

I think we all hold in our minds, whether consciously or not, an idea of the trajectory we expect our lives to inscribe. Mine was that I was going to live into my eighties, at least. But recently, long after the interchange I've just described, I spent time with a friend I hadn't seen for several years. Maxine asked me what had been most difficult for me, and I said it was having to face the likelihood of a shortened life span. She broke in, astonished: 'But we're 60! I've already lived much longer than I expected to. My mother died of cancer at 48 and I never thought I'd get anywhere near 60! Every year since 45 has been a bonus for me.'

I was rattled and upset after the conversation with Pat, but not for long. Just as Dr Lin's bombshell had pushed me into accepting the likelihood of mastectomy, this exchange pushed me towards acknowledging the reality of death. A few days later, when I saw Alan Stoker for my six-week check-up, I told him about my newly rising fears of recurrence and death and how difficult I was finding it to deal with them.

He was sympathetic, and gave me all the time I needed to talk, but he didn't give me reassurance. What he said was 'I can't tell you that it won't come back, no one could. These are facts of life, and you have to learn to accept them.'

Sunday 16 January

I'm beginning to get my head round the *fact* – the fact that there is no certainty now, and will never be again. No certainty of health, no certainty of long life. I always took that as given, but it is gone. I understand now that nothing is ever certain, not for anyone, not at any time. For every one of us, the next year, the next day, the next breath, could be the last one. This is always true. But I did not *know* it until now. Swamiji said on the phone this afternoon, 'You don't know it, you can't know it, until you've had to face death. You've faced it, now you can cope with it.' And I'm beginning to feel that I can. This is true knowledge, and it will be with me for the rest of my life. The knowledge itself I can handle. When it manifests as fear, I won't push it away. I'll say 'Hello fear', and cry, and let it go as soon as possible.

So Pat's remark has been useful. Like the shock Dr Lin gave me, it pushed me through to another stage, another realization: the absolute fact that there can be no certainty ever again. And of course here is another grain of truth, another lesson. I *am* thankful for my life. It has been a wonderful life with Klaus, and I have had six years of teaching and have helped a lot of people, and if it ends tomorrow or in a year or in five years I will still be thankful.

How can I sit here so calmly writing these things, writing about dying, leaving? Well, I'm only facing up to what billions of people before me have had to face up to. It's so much easier when you do face up to it! It changes your outlook. Everything becomes precious, every moment is important. Now I know. Every moment, every breath.

The old cliché – 'The only thing we have to fear is fear itself.' A couple of weeks ago, when the fear first started surfacing, and I was pushing it away, I had those terrible few days. And at that time I developed that pain around my left shoulder blade. Zena massaged it and it went away the next day, and maybe that was all there was to it. But just at that time I turned round and acknowledged my fear. It was a strange pain; I thought it odd that it should come on just when everything was getting better, physically, and I was afraid it might be due to the imbalance between my two sides. But it wasn't, and it hasn't come back. I considered the possibility that it might be emotional; I think it's quite likely it was caused by the suppression of the fear, the holding down. I say the pain was 'around my left shoulder blade'. And which organ is that near? My heart.

Thursday 20 January
I talked to Alan Thompson about the fear thing. He said 'You are being rational, rather than irrational', which is true. It's true that I don't feel fear very often. When I do, I can deal with it. I feel that I am moving towards real acceptance of the fact. Life has changed, it is a totally changed situation. It is how it is, now. And I think I really do accept it. In the last few days I have found myself thinking that I might not be around for another 30 years, that it might only be 20, or 10. What I want for whatever time there is left is to use it as well as I possibly can. I haven't accepted yet that it might be just one or two years, though!

But I know, from watching my thoughts, that I am coming round to acceptance of the *fact:* that time and life are finite, not unlimited, that we are all mortal – or, rather, that we all have mortal bodies which we have to leave at some time or other. I wish, of course, that mine had lasted better, and I wish I had looked after it better. But that is all past now: I can 'wish' without guilt. It is as it is now.

I would love to think that the care I am taking of myself now, that all I'm doing, will have the wonderful result that I get all the years that are possible, all the years I could have had had this not happened, and that I die of a heart attack or a stroke, quickly, sometime in my 80s, as I always assumed I would. But I suppose it's more probable that it will be cancer that gets me – and I can only hope it's a long time from now and that it's quick when it happens, and that I have friends who care about me and will see me out when it does. It's all in God's hands.

Friday 28 January
I seem to be developing acceptance of all sorts of things. I feel in good spirits, cheerful and contented, nearly all of the time. The facts are there. I know them well. And I feel good.

Terry said 'It's like the sun going behind a cloud. It will come out again.' I thought that was a lovely thing to say, and I thanked him, but when I thought about it afterwards it didn't seem to have anything to do with me. My sun hasn't gone behind a cloud. It's shining. He also said 'You'll stop thinking about it and stop being morbid after a while: that's inevitable.' I had been talking about my altered outlook, my growing acknowledgement of uncertainty and death. But I'm not morbid, I don't feel in the least morbid. I'm just looking at it all, facing the facts.

And yet, perhaps, it does strike people as morbid. I suppose I should be more careful – again, about what I say to whom. Perhaps most people would find talk of death and loss of certainty morbid. Except for Klaus and Swamiji. When I talk to Swamiji about death I get answers. I get illumination. And when I talk to Klaus I get acceptance. Today I said again: 'I always thought I'd be completely healthy till about 89 and then pop off quickly' and he said, chuckling, 'That was unreasonable.' And of course it was.

The loss of what I now think of as that false certainty is perhaps not really such a great loss. In its place now is a deeper knowledge of life and death. Acceptance.

Whatever happens, I know I will be given the strength to bear it. Suppose I did have a recurrence. There would be, I expect, a repeat of the first few days of this experience. The feelings would probably be the same: racking, intense, difficult to bear. But I would bear them, just as I bore them this time. It might be easier, having been through it once, or it might not. It's hard to imagine that the fear would have the same intensity, the same impact. But I could be wrong. However it might come, whatever the difficulties, the pain, the grief, the fear, I know I would be given all I need to cope with it. Suppose I were to die? Well, even that, I've started to face in a way. T said the other day: 'It seems a good way of preparing for death.' It will happen sometime. It may be sooner than I thought. I'm not saying I accept that, or that I delude myself it wouldn't be horrible at the time, but all the same, I have come to a deeper understanding, and I am further along the road to acceptance.

Monday 31 January
I wonder if, with the deeper knowledge I have now, I am going to be able to accept everything, anything that happens. Perhaps there will never be another trauma as shocking, as terrible, as the first: the disbelief, the anger, the terror, the grief. But as I said the other day, I know that whatever happens, the strength to deal with it will be given to me. And it strikes me now that what I'm afraid of, if I'm afraid of anything, is *the feelings themselves*, those powerful, overwhelming feelings. But I don't have to be afraid of feelings. I coped with them in November, and I will cope with them again if I have to. I coped by looking, observing, acknowledging, feeling.

I remember the first time I cried. It was Tuesday 2 November, the day after I took my lump to Alan Thompson. It was after the class at Pritchard's Road and I was sitting in the car in Victoria Park, finishing my sandwich, and the grief, suddenly, without warning, welled up from deep inside me, and the tears started. It took me by surprise, and I thought 'No, I don't want to feel this,' and I tried to stop it, but that lasted only a split second: then I let it come up, gave into it. I cried, and was astonished at the violence, the depth of it. I let the feeling out, and looked at it, and named it; I said to myself, 'This feels like grief.' I cried, and then stopped crying and went on to teach my class at Hugh Platt House.

I can't remember when I made the commitment to stay with myself, to look, to be honest, not to dodge or pretend. If it wasn't that Tuesday, it was very soon after, because by Thursday the 4th I was able to write: 'I mean to learn from it whatever it has to teach me' and 'The time has been useful. I have been able to adjust somewhat to the knowledge that something may be seriously wrong, and to look.' I was very clear. I am very clear. That was all I wanted. It is all that is necessary. Not positive, not fighting. Just clear. Looking. Seeing. That way clarity comes, understanding comes, knowledge comes, the deeper knowledge.

And if anything further happens, if there is a recurrence, I will cope with the feelings in the same way as I did then. They hold nothing that I need be afraid of. I am in a different place now. Something serious has happened to me, and I now know that it can, that it did, that it could again.

It took time, and help, and work, through both meditation and writing, to get to that point. But once I faced and accepted the reality of my own death, the truth of Sogyal Rinpoche's words was borne out by my experience. I stopped taking life for granted. It was like a mist clearing. Once it did, I could see more clearly, things came into sharper focus. It became easier to make decisions, to know what was important and what wasn't, what I wanted and didn't want to do, what was healing for me and what wasn't.

During this time I read a number of books about cancer, about coping with cancer. Most stressed the importance of 'a positive attitude' and exhorted me to 'fight', in the highly charged vocabulary of struggle, of war. I know that many cancer patients have found this helpful, but it wasn't right for me. Even at the beginning, while waiting for the diagnosis, when people urged me to 'be positive', I felt that I didn't want to be positive, I only wanted to be clear and steady, to be able to look at what was happening to me and stay in touch with it without panicking. Since then I have tried just to allow what is happening to happen, and to accept it as it is, as a process of healing and transformation, in the sure knowledge that it is all in God's hands, while being as much help and as little hindrance to the process as possible.

For example, I know that Carl and Stephanie Simonton's approach to visualization, described in their book *Getting Well Again*, is highly regarded and has helped a great many people. The Simontons, an American oncologist and psychologist, run the Cancer Counselling and Research Centre in Dallas, Texas, and have done a great deal of pioneering work with cancer patients. I knew of their work, and their book was one of the first I bought. I read it eagerly, and tried to practise the basic technique. I developed a visualization of myself assuming the Warrior pose, multiplying the image, and aiming and shooting thousands of sharp little arrows at cancer cells. But it didn't feel right. I couldn't see the point in fostering conflict, in meeting the so-called 'aggression' of cancer with more aggression. Somehow, despite the pressure I was under at the time (in the early days it's hard to distinguish between what is and isn't right for you amidst the welter of advice that pours in from people and books: it gets easier later) I simply knew these techniques weren't going to be relevant for me. Nor has *fighting* ever been a useful metaphor for me, then or since.

There are many paths to healing. Each of us has to find the one that is right for us, the one that meets us where we really are now, not where we wish we were, or think we ought to be. I'm not condemning the confrontational approach; I understand how it can be helpful for some. But I wonder whether it doesn't in fact operate as a kind of death-denial, and whether it isn't another guilt-trap waiting to be sprung: if it 'doesn't work', if the cancer recurs, you've somehow 'failed'. And supposing you die? Within such a context, dying becomes the ultimate failure.

Which of course it is not. As Bernie Siegel has pointed out, the mortality rate for the condition known as life is 100 per cent.

I know that the Simontons and others who teach these visualization techniques are aware of these dangers and have tried to help people avoid them, but I believe they remain. If we perceive cancer as a malevolent aggressor, and our experience of cancer as an armed conflict, a battle with a deadly enemy, we are bound to feel we have failed if we 'lose the battle', if the technique does not yield the longed-for, striven-for result.

I perceive cancer differently. It is part of me, part of my experience of life. I surrendered to it and accepted it as a teaching at the start, and I continue to do so. If, instead, I were to regard it as an enemy and fight it, I would be fighting a part of myself. I would be setting up a conflict which, inevitably, 'I' could only lose. Through having cancer I have learned to look at illness and death not as a battlefield, and certainly not as failure, but as opportunities for spiritual unfoldment, growth and change. Along the path I am travelling, fighting isn't a help.

What helps me is yoga: breath awareness, movement, meditation and relaxation; paying closer attention to my nutrition, reading the *Bhagavad Gita*, the *Upanishads* and other spiritually nourishing books, friendship, journal-writing, love. All these help: these, and the commitment I made at the beginning to go through the experience of cancer, not to circumvent it; to keep my eyes open and meet it face to face, not to duck it; to take it in; and to look clearly and steadily at every facet of that experience and at every feeling, every issue it put before me.

The big issue, of course, is death. Of all the things that cancer is giving me, the most valuable is this growing understanding of the nature of death, not only as an inevitable fact of life, but as a natural part of it.

A life-threatening illness offers us the challenge of changing and healing our lives. It offers us the opportunity to acknowledge death and prepare for it before it happens.

Jean Klein says:

> *Illness and death are an opportunity, par excellence, to clarify the fundamental error of our existence... Illness is a gift, a gift to realize more quickly what we are not. It gives us an opportunity which should not be refused: to be what we are.* [3]

I *know*, now, that my body is not going to last forever, that sooner or later I shall be letting go of it. This knowledge is giving my life a sharper focus, a richer texture. And it is helping me prepare myself for death, so that when the time comes I have a better chance of not going out in blind terror, kicking and screaming, but consciously, peacefully, willingly.

I have come to what I hope is a full and open awareness and acceptance of reality, including the reality of death. This is, of course, a continuing, probably a life-long process. But I have at least begun to explore how the experience of cancer can be used to prepare oneself for death, and to discover how much more helpful it is (and what a relief it is) to acknowledge mortality than to ignore and deny it.

It's denial that creates fear, and tightens its grip on us. Epictetus was surely right to say that we are disturbed by the views we take of things and not of the things themselves, and that 'the terror consists in our notion of death'. Once we look clearly at the reality, once we accept the challenge cancer offers to face death and prepare for it, we can begin to let go of the fear of dying and embrace the challenge of changing and healing our lives while we are still here.

My next-door neighbour observed not long ago: 'Cancer is quite a good way to go, now that pain is more easily controlled. It gives you time to put things in order.' I was only a little surprised to find myself agreeing. It is quite likely that it will be cancer I die from – whether sooner or later – and that prospect no longer horrifies me. I used to think, when I heard of someone dying quickly of a stroke or heart failure, that 'that was the way to go': shocking and painful for the person's loved ones, but a blessing for the individual; and I was sure that was how I wanted to go.

Not any more. Before I die, I want to know that it is going to happen. I want time: time to accept that death is near, time to deal with any unfinished business, to heal anything that needs healing in my relationships with others, to say goodbye to my friends, to make the transition between this stage of being and the next. I want to experience that transition and welcome it fully, openly. I want those weeks or months to complete my healing, to heal into death.

The Swiss writer Peter Noll kept a journal during the nine months between his diagnosis with bladder cancer and his death. Published in English translation as *In the Face of Death*, it includes a short 'sermon' he wrote to be read at his funeral, in which he says:

> Not only the Christians but particularly non-Christians from Seneca and Montaigne to Heidegger, were of the opinion that life made more sense if one thought of death rather than shoved the thought of it aside or repressed it. They also said that it was easier to die if one thought about death throughout one's life rather than being surprised by it. I have found all of this to be true. I had time to acquaint myself with death. That is the true benefit of dying from cancer, which everybody fears so much.
>
> I knew that my time was briefer than I had imagined earlier and that I had thought too little about time and its limits before. I felt a great deal of sadness but also true joyousness and, astonishingly, no despair. We naturally are aware that we must die, yet we still act as if life would continue forever, as if death applied only to others...
>
> What ought to change in our lives if we think of death? Much, but not everything. We shall gain a wiser heart, as the psalmist says. We shall use time more carefully, be more considerate of others, more loving, more patient – and above all more free. No one can take more from us than our lives, and this will be taken from us anyway. This thought generates a feeling of freedom, like a breath of fresh air...
>
> Because of my experiences over the last several months, I can say to you that the thought of death makes life more precious. [4]

Ailsa lent me this truthful and beautifully written book a few months after my mastectomy, but it was too soon. I had to put it to one side: I couldn't yet tolerate this brave, intelligent man's unflinching look at death. Now, I can, and it will be clear from everything I have said that I share Peter Noll's outlook and his feelings.

I have not yet had to face what he has had to face. But for me, too, the thought of death has made life more precious. And the acknowledgement of death has been liberating. The journey toward this awareness has been a healing journey. I live, reasonably comfortably, with the awareness that cancer, now that I have had it, is more likely than not to be the cause of my eventual death. If that happens, whenever it happens, I trust that cancer, which has already helped me to heal my life, helped me to live a fuller, more conscious life, will then yield me a more conscious death, a healing death.

4   Please Don't Blame the Victim

Life is too wonderfully complex for a simple statement like 'you create your own reality' to be simply true.

Treya Killam Wilber

An astonishing number of people who get cancer blame themselves for getting it, and I was no exception: my first impulse was to reproach myself. Instantly, I started looking for all the reasons why I might have got cancer, tormenting myself with recalling all the things I'd done that might have helped cause it, all the things I'd not done that might have helped avoid it.

Does everyone do this? Or do perhaps only women do it? I don't know. But I do know that it is the most unhelpful thing we can do. Guilt, self-punishment and self-blame can only intensify the distress of a cancer diagnosis. They depress the immune system, impede recovery and healing, and make it much harder to cope with all the realities, all the practicalities, all the decisions and difficulties that lie ahead.

Looking back on the catalogue of guilts, of all the thoughts and actions and neglects I blamed myself for, I'm appalled to think that I gave myself such a hard time. Fortunately it didn't last long. Fortunately, I had help: Klaus, Swamiji, and several sensible friends told me emphatically to stop it.

Swamiji said 'It doesn't matter what you did or why it happened. Probably you didn't do anything, and even if you did there's no point in worrying about it now. What matters now is getting yourself right. What matters now is what you do with this experience, how you *use* it.' I came to see that it isn't necessarily helpful to rake over the coals of the past; that when a bombshell like cancer falls upon us we need to look ahead, not back, and consider the changes we may need to make in our lives now.

The first thing I scolded myself for was not having taken my lump to the doctor as soon as I discovered it. That had happened while I was lying in bed one night early in October: turning over to go to sleep on my left side, my hand brushed my breast and came in contact with the lump: round, hard, not small, unmistakably *there*. I knew it was there. I knew what it might be. But it took me a full four weeks to open my mouth and say to Klaus on the morning of Monday 1 November, 'I have a lump.'

'Where?'

'In my breast.'

'You have to go to the doctor.'

'I know.'

For several days before that, I had been opening my mouth to speak, and closing it again, like a fish, unable to utter the words that would have to be followed by action, the words that would make the horror real.

When Caroll arrived at the class on Tuesday evening I told her, and she said 'When I came into the room just now I knew you were going to tell me something I didn't want to hear. A fortnight ago I dreamed you were trying to tell me something, *and you kept opening and closing your mouth but not saying anything.* I've known you had something to tell me ever since. And I almost asked you – but I didn't want to know.'

In hospital one of the nurses, Louise, pointed out that during those four weeks I was beginning to acknowledge that something might be seriously wrong with me, and she made me see how useful that time had been. 'If you hadn't done that then,' she said, 'you might have been in a terrible state now.' I'm not recommending my delaying tactics. My tumour was well-differentiated (not very aggressive), so the month's delay hadn't made any difference, especially as everything proceeded so quickly once I did start the ball rolling, but it could have made a difference to a more aggressive cancer. The sooner a lump or other suspicious symptom is investigated, the better.

Louise's insight helped me let go of that bit of guilt. There were others. My first journal entry was full of it.

Thursday 4 November
When I found the lump, I avoided realizing. First I told myself my fingers were wrong. Then I hoped it would go away. When I finally let the worry surface I almost decided I would lie when asked 'When did you notice it?' But of course I didn't. And everyone has reassured me: 'We all do it.' So perhaps I'm not

uniquely stupid. Anyway, I did it and that's that. If it's cancer, and far advanced, I've made it worse by not dealing with it immediately, but it's done. But I still feel I have been silly, and that I am to blame.

I also blame myself for not having taken better care of my body, which is now possibly breaking down. For having abused my strong constitution by not eating as well as I ought to have. I know that people who do everything right still get cancer; as Lynne says, some do and some don't, and perhaps whatever I ate or didn't eat had nothing to do with it. And perhaps I don't have cancer. But if I do, it will take a lot of rationalizing and forgiving to stop holding myself responsible. This body should have lasted better; it had everything going for it and nothing wrong with it except what I've done to it.

There are times when I look at the worst option, and am overwhelmed with grief. Grief for Klaus, if he is to be left alone. Grief for all the work I wanted to do and should have done and now won't have the time to do. And I can't comfort myself by thinking it's perhaps God's will I should go now, because God didn't want me to abuse my body. I should have had all the time I needed, and if it is being taken away from me, it's me who has taken it. I don't hold God responsible, I am responsible, and I apologize to God from the bottom of my heart.

I hadn't 'abused' my body; the force of my language simply reflects the intensity of the guilt that overcame me at the time. For a while, I used every available stick to beat myself up with.

Friday 5 November
I blame myself for having abused my strong constitution. My body should have lasted the course, and it would have had I taken better care of it. How stupid can one be. Stella said, 'Don't blame yourself'. And I know it could have happened anyway, and does happen all the time to people who do eat better than I do, and I also know it isn't going to help me to blame myself. So I will try to stop it.

But guilt and blame seemed called for at the time, and it was some time before I was able to drop them.

Now I know, and would say to anyone who faces a cancer diagnosis, that when we have cancer, or any serious illness, all that matters is our healing. Whatever may have happened in the past, what matters now is that we try to bring our life into balance now. What matters is that we forgive ourselves and co-operate with ourselves to enhance our immune system and bring our inner healing powers into play.

In *Peace, Love and Healing* Bernie Siegel says:

> *Those of you who feel guilt because you believe you have caused your own illnesses, or who feel like failures if you cannot cure them, are giving your healing system a destructive message. You must let go of feelings of guilt and failure so that, unencumbered by these negative messages, you can utilize to the fullest your innate healing capacities.*[5]

We do need to come to some understanding of what has happened to us, and if we suspect some habit or behaviour or thought pattern of having contributed to the disease, it makes sense to try to change it. For example, the links between smoking and certain types of cancer and coronary heart disease are now very well established. So if we smoke, it would clearly be sensible to make the connection, and try to stop smoking. Or, if we suspect that stress has contributed to our becoming ill, it makes sense to do whatever we can to change the stressful situations in our lives, and at the same time enhance our ability to deal with stress by learning and practising breathing and relaxation techniques. This is straightforward, common sense. We need to take responsibility for ourselves and our future lives now, and illness presents us with the challenge and the opportunity of doing so.

This isn't the same thing as self-blame. There is a difference between abdicating responsibility and forgiving oneself, between reproaching oneself for the past and taking responsibility for one's life and health and healing in the present, as I was beginning to discover.

Monday 27 December
And now it occurs to me that it may actually not be so important to 'dig', to find out 'why this happened', that it may be more helpful simply to accept, and to accept fully, that it did happen, to accept whatever I 'did to cause it' or 'didn't do to avoid it', and forgive myself. And to affirm that, whatever the cause of it, for whatever reason it happened, I do not 'blame' myself. Not going on a guilt trip about it isn't denying truth, isn't a false absolution.

For I do take responsibility for it, and that is something different from blame, and I do that now, even without 'knowing why', even without that particular insight (which might turn out to be rather superficial anyway, even if I happened upon it in any conscious, deliberate 'digging' I might do). I take responsibility for myself, for me, the whole of me, including my cancer.

I do accept. I think I do forgive myself. I do take responsibility for it all, and I don't blame myself.

I just want to *be*, I don't want to delve, dig, grapple, do detective work, undo myself, undress myself, try to find things out, strain for 'answers'. I've done too much of that in the past. I trust this process that is going on now, whatever it is, wherever it is taking me, and I don't think I want to interfere with it. Something has been planted, and it should be allowed to take root, grow, flower, watched over by God and nourished and gently tended by me, all that I am, all that I've become, all that I am becoming. It can't be right to peek and pry, lift corners to see what's underneath, tear off strips of skin, pick scabs, force zips. No. I wish to continue as I began, seven weeks ago, riding on the tide of love and strength that has supported me, borne me along, from the beginning. Where I am now, delving, digging, poking, has no relevance.

If what I am, if what I have grown to be in all these years of working and learning and living and reflecting and contemplating is not enough, then so be it. But I think it is, I think it will be.

So, helped by Klaus and Swamiji and my friends, who were all thinking more clearly than I was at that time, I let go of guilt and blame.

During my healing process almost everyone gave the non-judging love and support I needed, but there were a few people whose views on illness pulled on my 'guilt strings' and made things more difficult for me at first.

There is a 'New Age' theory that we 'create our own reality', including our illnesses. The idea is that we 'choose' to be ill, that we bring our illnesses upon ourselves, and that we do this because we 'need' our illnesses and therefore make them happen. People with this outlook tend to ask questions like 'Why did you create this illness in your life?' The theory is widely held, and, unfortunately, laid on patients, by many practitioners of complementary therapies who ought to know better.

I believe that this theory is simplistic and dangerous and without foundation. However well-intentioned its proponents may be, it operates as an underhanded way of blaming the victim while purporting to help. It's an irresponsible distortion of the truth that we can use our inner strength and our innate healing powers to help heal ourselves. It transposes this truth into the glib assumption, for which there is no evidence, that psychological and personality factors constitute the major, even the sole, cause of illness.

Of course our thoughts affect and influence our reality (without thought to precede it, there would be no action, no speech). But to maintain that they and they alone *create* it indicates an egocentric, even a narcissistic view of life. The notion that we can manipulate reality in this way suggests delusions of grandeur, a presumption of omnipotence. In enthroning the individual at the absolute centre of the universe it ignores everyone else in it, as well as the enormous variety of factors that affect our lives over which we do not have control.

(The theory of karma is often invoked by the 'you create your reality/illness' brigade. This is not the place for a full discussion of karma, except to say that it is widely misunderstood. Karma, the universal law of cause and effect, is a majestic concept that encompasses the workings of the entire creation. It is holistic. It is not, and should not be exploited as, a narrow-minded excuse for blaming individuals for their misfortunes because 'It's their karma.')

I believe that we have control over our own attitudes and thoughts, and that this empowers us to take full, grown-up responsibility for ourselves. When illness arrives, it enables us to rise to its challenge and take action to make the changes we need to make in our lives. But it takes only a moment's reflection to realize that over the external influences on what happens to us, including our illnesses – the environmental, political, educational and social influences – we quite obviously do not have control.

Treya Killam Wilber, who died in 1991, five years after developing metastatic breast cancer, wrote in her journal (quoted in her husband Ken Wilber's excellent book *Grace and Grit*) of the narrowness and restrictiveness of the 'you create your reality' view:

> *Unravelling the past too easily degenerates into a kind of self-blame*
> *which makes it harder, not easier, to make healthy, conscious choices in*

the present. I am also very aware of the many other factors which are largely beyond my conscious or unconscious control. We are all, thankfully, part of a much larger whole. I like being aware of this, even though it means I have less control. We are all too interconnected, both with each other and with our environment – life is too wonderfully complex – for a simple statement like 'you create your own reality' to be simply true. The belief that I control or create my own reality actually attempts to tip me out of the rich, complex, mysterious and supportive context of my life. It attempts, in the name of control, to deny the web of relationships which nurtures me and each of us daily.[6]

The 'you create your reality' theory may have started life as a useful corrective to theories of illness, such as the 'germ' theory, which take no account of the field in which illness operates, and allow no latitude for personal responsibility. But it has gone too far. It would be laughable if it was not responsible for doing so much harm. But it does enormous harm. It's an insidious form of victim-blaming that heaps guilt on sick people who are already struggling under a heavy load. It feeds into their inherent tendency to blame themselves for their illness, reinforcing their guilt and fear and sense of powerlessness, creating additional anxiety and impeding recovery and healing.

There is a great deal that we don't know. Life and illness and death are indeed far too complex and mysterious, and raise far too many deep questions, for there to be pat, simple answers to any of them. Anyone who thinks that it is helpful to tell a person with cancer 'You create your own reality; therefore you created your illness' should think again.

People with cancer, indeed, sufferers from any illness, already feel victimized by their illness, and are not helped by being additionally victimized by the opinions or beliefs of others. They have enough to cope with without having laid on them the sanctimonious judgement that they brought it on themselves. The implication is that if you don't accept that judgement (which means granting the person who delivers it the right to judge you) and 'get to the bottom of' whichever of your psychological flaws 'caused' the illness, you will have a recurrence of it.

No one has the knowledge, the competence or the right to pass such a judgement on anyone else.

If you are ill, and a friend or practitioner offers 'help' in this spirit, you may be able to protect yourself from their approach by understanding clearly that it is a fallacy and that it can hurt you.

If you are the friend or relative of someone who is ill, or their practitioner, and if you imagine you are helping them by disclosing your views on their personality and their psychological history and quirks, or analysing where you think they've gone wrong, or encouraging them to 'take a good look at themselves', you might like to consider that this is not for you to do. It isn't compassionate or healing or loving, it's judging. It's setting yourself above them. You may think you are helping them, but your approach to their situation will make them shrink from you – that is, if they are able to protect themselves. If they aren't, you are likely to hinder their healing.

(The judgemental attitude we may display towards those who are suffering from cancer, or any other fear-inspiring disease such as Aids, or any physical or psychological abnormality, actually tells us more about ourselves than it does about the person on whom we are passing judgement. At the very least, it tells us that our attitude is judgemental rather than supportive.)

One evening, while talking on the phone to an acupuncturist acquaintance, I asked him what he knew about fluid accumulation. I was having some difficulty with this. My drains had come out a bit too soon, lymphatic fluid kept building up around the wound and under my armpit, and I was having to go back to the hospital several times a week to have it drained. It was very uncomfortable, and now a mild infection had set in.

I had asked him for an answer to a specific question about a physical phenomenon, and had hoped he would be able to tell me how long I might expect to have to endure it. What he said was: 'If I were you, Julie, I would use this time to dig deep into what caused the whole thing and find out why it happened, what you did to cause it.'

Those whose views on illness lead them to talk to sick people in this way tend to be very sure of the rightness of their views. They may mean well, but they don't realize how much guilt and self-blame they cause. (I doubt that anyone who has experienced real illness could continue to hold those views, even if they held them before.) Spinning facile theories about why their mother or spouse or friend or patient developed cancer ('She thought too much about others and not enough about herself', 'She couldn't express her anger', 'He couldn't handle stress') is simply not helpful. The point isn't whether or not such a conjecture is true, but that it comes over to the sick person – even if it is not directly expressed – as a judgement, a violation, and adds to their distress.

We all – doctors, nurses, carers, practitioners of complementary therapies, families, friends, even casual acquaintances – stand in a position to influence the healing of someone who is ill. That influence can be helpful or it can be unhelpful. Love and empathy and kindness freely given can nourish the springs of healing. Judgement, however well-intentioned, can dry them up and do great, sometimes irreparable, damage.

There may be people reading this, including practitioners, who hold the theory I have been attempting to discredit: well-intentioned individuals devoted to the welfare of their friends and patients. I hope they, and any others involved in the care and support of the sick, will consider what I have said, and try to think themselves into the shoes of the people they are trying to help. (They might recall the Native American saying 'Never judge a man till you have walked for two weeks in his moccasins.')

When parts of this chapter appeared in *Yoga and Health*, it was obvious from the response that I am not alone in seeing the dangers in the New Age view that persuades people that they create their reality and their illnesses.

Unfortunately, it would seem that the people most likely to impose this particular belief on their patients and clients are to be encountered among practitioners of complementary therapies. Perhaps those who do, do so from an incomplete understanding of energy, of healing, of certain great laws of life that govern the workings of the universe, such as karma, or simply from insensitivity.

And yet, complementary, or as I would rather call it, holistic medicine is a rich field of potential help to the cancer patient. Acupuncture, the Alexander technique, aromatherapy, herbal medicine, homoeopathy, massage, naturopathy, nutritional therapy, osteopathy and chiropractic, reflexology, shiatsu, spiritual healing and yoga are all holistic. They all work with energies, and they all treat the patient as a whole person, rather than as a collection of symptoms, a tumour with a person attached. They have a great deal to offer anyone with cancer.

I would certainly not advise anyone with cancer to reject the orthodox treatments offered by the cancer specialists and rely entirely on the holistic therapies. They are what their other name indicates: complementary. But we should know about them and avail ourselves of their help wherever appropriate. The orthodox cancer treatments – surgery, radiotherapy, chemotherapy – are aggressive external attacks on cancer. Chemotherapy especially, which kills healthy cells as well as cancer cells, depresses the immune system. The holistic therapies work from inside, to enhance the immune system, restore the balance of energies and encourage healing. If adjuvant treatments such as chemotherapy are advised, they can help in coping with the side effects and in revitalizing the immune system. Through every stage of the illness the holistic therapies can do much to improve the quality of life, and when death itself is near, they can ease the passage.

But we have to choose our helpers with care. When we are ill, we are likely to be more sensitive than usual, open and vulnerable to the suggestions and offers of help that flow towards us from all sides. We need to learn to distinguish between those that are likely to be helpful to us and those that are not.

In both orthodox Western medicine, and in holistic medicine, there are practitioners who are sincere, humble, aware of their limitations and the limits of their technical knowledge, and who genuinely wish to be of use to humanity. These are the real healers: they work with compassion, and with respect for the first principle of healing: that the healer shall do no harm. They understand that the energy which heals us is a universal energy, and that they are being used as channels for that energy. Most of them would say that they deem it a privilege to be where they are, to be used in this way, to be of service. Others, who have a different vocabulary (orthodox surgeons, for example), might not say it in precisely this way, but they show that they know it through their actions.

But there are others, in both the orthdox and holistic fields, who have put themselves where they are because they covet the superiority their position gives them over others, because it gives them power. Driven by ego, they believe, mistakenly, that the energy they are using is 'their' energy. These are the ones – however skilled, however knowledgeable they are – whose treatment may not be helpful to us.

We need to discriminate. Then we can seek the true healers and recognize them when we find them, and protect ourselves from those who are simply power-driven. The former will join forces with us and help us to heal, understanding that the journey is our journey and that they are there only to facilitate it. The latter are unfortunately all too likely to persuade us that they are in charge of the journey, and to lay trips on us that will trigger our guilt and block our healing.

In a relationship with such a therapist we may be led to feel that our healing process is the responsibility of the therapist, when, of course, it is our own. The effect of such manipulation of the therapeutic relationship, whether or not it is consciously sought, is to disempower the patient while empowering the therapist. In seeking healing, we need to be aware that this can happen, and be alert for the danger signals.

The story of my own experience with a practitioner of Traditional Chinese Medicine to whom I went for help, illustrates the point.

I went to N for three months for herbal treatment and acupuncture, and then brought my relationship with him to an end because I could see that it was not healing for me.

N belonged to the 'you created your illness' school. 'Cancer isn't something that comes in the window', he said, at our first consultation early in December, soon after I left hospital. 'It's *you*. It's nothing to do with diet or the environment, it's all to do with your emotions. It's something you grow.' At that stage I wasn't inclined to question this point of view: I didn't know enough about cancer, and hadn't yet entirely shaken off self-blame. But as I began to discover the difference between self-blame and self-responsibility, as I began to take responsibility for my own healing, as I took the measure of the challenge and the opportunity my illness was offering me, and as I learned more about breast cancer, which is a disease with many causes, not one, I realized that N's treatment wasn't helping me.

I stayed with it for three months. When I was with him, I felt like an ill person going for treatment; I would arrive feeling well and full of energy, and would leave 45 minutes later feeling discouraged and low-spirited. I felt he was judging me. At first I took the blame, supposing my powers of perception to be clouded by some sort of post-operative paranoia, but I saw in time that he really *was* judgemental.

The problem wasn't in the herbs or the needling. N was an experienced and highly regarded practitioner, and the TCM system itself, 5,000 years old, well tried and well attested, is soundly-based and sophisticated. The problem was in N's outlook and in the relationship that developed between us, which I realized, as my understanding of illness and healing grew, wasn't a healing relationship.

N was dogmatic, and somewhat rigid. He had an unvarying set of questions to ask me each time I came, and if I raised anything that wasn't on his agenda he became restless and impatient and frequently cut me short. I came to feel that he simply wasn't listening, and stopped trying. He had strong views on orthodox Western medicine and was much given to making scornful remarks about 'the men in white coats'. When I was prescribed antibiotics for the wound infection, his reaction was an explosive 'Damn! You should have told me. I would have given you something better,' and he frequently exhorted me: 'You don't *have* to do what they say!'

I felt that he was disparaging the good, compassionate treatment I had had from Alan Stoker, and setting up a conflict between his own treatment and that of my 'orthodox Western doctors'. But I didn't want conflict, I wanted the best of both worlds. I wanted any treatment I had, now or in the future, from him or Alan Stoker or any other practitioner, to be in the full context of myself and my responsibility for my body, my healing and my life, and I wanted any decisions I made to be respected.

Writing about this experience after it was over, I contrasted it with my experience with Alan Stoker, who was, as I recognized from the moment I met him, one of the real healers.

Monday 21 March

Healing is something that happens within a relationship. The relationship between the healer and the healed is a two-way process, a sharing of the healing energy. In a truly healing relationship, mutual acceptance, trust and faith have either been there from the start, or allowed and encouraged to grow. All of that was there with Alan, who had 'only' Western techniques of diagnosis and surgery to offer, but it wasn't there with N, with all his knowledge of the ancient and beautiful system of TCM. I tried to build it with him, but it wasn't possible to do it. I never had to try with Alan, it was all just always *there*.

So, here is this surgeon, one of that species reviled by N, who stuck at least a dozen needles in me, what with tests and fluid-draining, and cut off my breast, and prescribed me antibiotics when the wound was infected – and with him I felt, and I feel, and I know I am, *healed*. It is a healing relationship. Full stop. He always made me feel less ill, better, good.

Healing is *there*; healing power, healing energy, is all around us, God-given. Whatever we do, whether it's surgery, or massage, or yoga teaching, or spiritual healing, or shiatsu or TCM we can tap into it, be used as a channel for it. But we have to trust it and open ourselves to it. And we have to discipline ourselves to be worthy of it, and able to handle it. N could do that if he wanted to, but he doesn't want to: he doesn't trust it. 'I don't call myself a healer,' he says. He trusts his academic learning, his vast knowledge of TCM, the intellect that has enabled him to grasp it and use it, and the medicine (even of the medicine, he says 'faith in it is a non-parameter.') But he doesn't trust himself, or God.

Apart from the harm it inflicts on individuals, I believe that the 'you create your reality/illness' theory has another, perhaps ultimately more serious effect: it diverts attention and energy away from the real physical causes of physical illness, and from the political, environmental and social issues around cancer. It may be easier, for example (and it is certainly cheaper) to encourage people to think they got cancer because they thought the wrong thoughts, or failed to be sufficiently 'happy', than it would be to clean up the environment or tackle food pollution, or fund research into the causes and prevention of cancer and muster the political will to act on its findings.

A broader, more compassionate view of illness is needed, one that accepts that we simply don't know all the causes, that serious illnesses like cancer can strike anyone at any time, and that it may not be useful to dig ourselves up in the search for causes and blame ourselves for creating them. It's more helpful to look forward, to accept illness as a challenge, and to use it as an opportunity to change whatever in our lives needs changing, whether or not it may have contributed to our illness. To work our way through the experience of illness to the healing, the truths, the rewards, that lie at its core. And, eventually, to share those truths, those rewards, that healing, with others.

Sometimes, sick people find that others step back from them. This can come as a shock, but if we are prepared for it and understand that it usually arises from fear, it will be less distressing.

There are many reasons why people may not want to come close to a cancer patient. Their fear of cancer may make it difficult for them, or they may just not know what to do or say to help. Or, knowing that their views on illness are different from ours, they may move away from us out of thoughtfulness, so as not to disturb our peace of mind. We can't expect everyone to share our beliefs and our understanding of illness and healing, any more than we can expect everyone to be able to help.

Cancer changes everything, including our relationships with others, and we have to accept this as we accept all the other changes. Some friends come closer, others step back; some bonds loosen, others grow stronger. That is life. The generous support I was given, the love and the care, have deepened old friendships and allowed new ones to flourish, and this has more than compensated for the distance that arose between me and one of my friends.

At first I didn't understand. Then, knowing her to be an adherent of the 'you create your illness' theory, I began to wonder if the explanation for her withdrawal was to be found there. Months later, when I was able to talk to her about what had happened, she confirmed my early speculation. She said, 'I know we don't see eye to eye on these matters, and I knew that if I came to see you, you wouldn't want to hear my views.'

In *Peace, Love and Healing* Bernie Siegel says: 'Viewing disease as a sign of personal inadequacy or culpability is both cruel and false.' He quotes a letter from a woman cancer patient which eloquently expresses what I know from my own experience to be the truth:

> *Some of the things that people have said to me in the past two years have been really cruel, even though they were intended to be caring. One friend suggested that I must have spent my time in therapy avoiding, because if I'd been working I wouldn't have got sick. A number of people reminded me that we create our own reality and therefore I should look at why I created my cancer. And this summer a workshop leader told me that 'it wasn't enough to cut off my breast and put a bunch of chemicals in my body'. Until I could say 'I created my own cancer' and be full with that, I would get sick again.*
>
> *God's gifts sometimes come in strange packages. My experiences have helped me to get really clear that I am not in control of the outcome. I am in charge of my attitude and what I give to my life and how I treat my body. But I am not in control of the outcome of my illness. It has been a very long time growing to this understanding, and letting go of my sense of failure. I kept turning back on myself, thinking that I must be doing something wrong, or I wasn't trying hard enough, or maybe I was somehow sabotaging myself. Because after all, if I was doing it right I wouldn't be sick, be in pain, bleed, etc.*
>
> *Please, please take care not to set a new standard for failure. So much of what you say offers hope for a better way of living. But it is so important to work for goals which are attainable. I can hope for a miracle but I can't make one happen and I'm not a failure or a bad person if one doesn't happen. I can work for peace of mind. I can choose to live each moment fully. I can choose to love and be loving. But – at least in my experience – when I choose not to have side effects from chemotherapy, not bleed, not be in pain, shrink my tumour, drive cancer from my body,*

not have a recurrence – these are outcomes I'm less in charge of attaining.

You remembered to point out that the mortality rate (for the condition known as life) is 100 per cent. Please also encourage us to hope and work for the best outcome and then to love and accept ourselves no matter what happens. When the outcomes are less than we want, loving ourselves is even more important. The Universe/God will provide everything I need – not everything I want. So teach that when I don't get what I want I'm not a failure – and I'm not necessarily doing something wrong. As a patient I really needed to hear that. And I needed for some of my friends to hear that too.

Bernie Siegel comments:

I hope this message gets through, not only to patients and their loved ones, but to doctors, too. I hope therapists, doctors, family members and friends never make people feel like failures, or make them feel that they are still ill because they have not changed enough, achieved enough or made significant enough existential shifts… the outcome of the disease may be beyond the limits of our power, and we must learn, as the writer of this letter did, where those limits lie. But that doesn't mean abdicating all responsibility. Responsibility and guilt are not the same things. Neither are disease and failure.[7]

I too hope that this message gets through.

In *Healing into Life and Death*, Stephen Levine says:

We have seen among the 'very healed' many that nonetheless experience illness. Many holy women and men, many saints and adepts, bodied with disease. Even 'enlightenment' does not preclude the possibility of suffering in the body. Indeed, most of my spiritual teachers have experienced illness of one sort or another – Neem Karoli Baba, known as Maharaji, suffered what appeared to be a heart attack; Ramana Maharshi died of cancer, as did Nisargadatta. Suzuki Roshi also died of cancer, as did Ramakrishna and Vivekananda…

Experiencing the illnesses of such spiritual friends and teachers, noting their remarkable responses, has helped us to let go of any half truth or concept about the cause of illness or what true healing might be.[8]

When illness comes, to any of us, the best we can do is accept it as part of the life process, and trust that process. Judgements have no place in that process.

As human beings, we are bound by a sacred trust: to avoid doing harm. In yoga it is called *ahimsa*, or non-injury, and it means that no harm should be done to any living creature, either in action, speech or thought. We should honour that trust, and try to encourage healing wherever and whenever we can. And we should know that with the trust comes a responsibility: not to judge our fellow beings but to act towards them with compassion and love.

5   Secret Miracles

There are secret miracles at work
That only Time will bring forth.

Ben Okri – *African Elegy*

Cancer, as therapists have pointed out, has a great deal in common with bereavement. Certainly the shock and grief one experiences at first are strikingly similar. I remember thinking, the first time I cried, 'This feels like grief.' I hadn't felt anything remotely like it since my father had died ten years earlier, and I recognized it at once.

'Coping with it', 'digesting it', 'assimilating it', 'coming to terms with it', 'processing it': whatever words you use to describe it, dealing with cancer is a long-term process, with the same recognizable stages as are said to characterize bereavement. Elisabeth Kubler-Ross has described these as shock, denial, anger, grief and bargaining, and says that they all have to be undergone to come through to acceptance and healing. This cannot be done quickly; it takes time, and we need to give ourselves that time.

Recovering from the shock of diagnosis and treatment is only the beginning of getting through the immensity of cancer. It takes much longer to comprehend the full extent of the physical and psychological trauma of surgery, longer still to take in the long-term implications of cancer and absorb the changes it brings about. We can't start doing all this until we are ready to do it. The mind has an ingenious way of protecting us from knowledge we aren't ready to take in. It lets in only what we can bear, a little at a time. The real journey begins only when physical recovery is complete.

My reaction was probably typical. After the anxious, exhausting weeks that led up to surgery I entered hospital calm and fearless, having accepted that I was going to lose a breast, impatient to be rid of the tumour, and confident that once it had been removed I would 'be all right' and never have to worry about cancer again.

How could I have thought this? Did I really know so little about cancer? I don't know: I can't remember what I knew before. What I do know is that my mind was operating like a very fine, tiny lens opening, seeing only what it could bear to see, letting in nothing that I could not yet tolerate seeing. Being anaesthetized, being cut, losing a breast, being in pain for a while – I had accepted all this and could cope with it, but not with the knowledge that cancer, the reality of cancer, the possibility of cancer recurring, the possibility of dying from cancer, would be with me for the rest of my life.

When the junior house doctor did my admission interview, she said 'We'll have the results of the pathology in a few days, and then we can talk to you about your prognosis.' She had apparently assessed me as rational and well-informed and ready to hear those words, 'pathology', 'prognosis', but I didn't want to hear them. I asked her – rather belligerently, as I recall to my shame – what she meant. I told her that as I understood it, this was it, that after the operation there would be nothing more for me to worry about. The poor girl realized her blunder and quickly changed the subject.

I had entered hospital totally focused on surgery. The surgeon's knife was going to excise my tumour. I looked forward to that as to a rite of purification. My body would be cleansed of cancer, and that would be the end of it. Prognosis? What was that? I wasn't going to have cancer any more: I would get better, get back to my life, to my work, and never have to think about cancer again. My future was clear, assured. Little did I know – and it was many weeks before I did know.

I came out of the anaesthetic several hours before I was expected to, and was out of bed the same evening, telling everyone how fine I felt. And I did. I was euphoric. The operation was over, I was alive, and the relief, after all the anxiety of the previous three weeks, was enormous. The adrenaline was flowing. I thought I had come to terms with everything. I thought that was all there was to 'getting over cancer'.

I didn't know yet that you don't 'get over cancer'. Nevertheless, I was thrilled to find myself bouncing back so quickly. Everyone who came to see me was amazed at how well I looked and seemed and sounded, and was happy for me, and that, it seemed, was that.

As soon as I was home, I asked Alan Thompson to refer me to a good physiotherapist and focused my energies on regaining the movement of my arm and shoulder. I thought of nothing else for the next six weeks, and once that was accomplished with Zena Schofield's help, I thought once again, 'There, that's it, I've done it, I'm ready to get back to my life now.'

But it was only then that what had happened really hit me, and I began to comprehend the full magnitude of it. Bit by bit, it all began to sink in, and letting it all in was a sort of shock-absorbing process that took several months and all my energy. And that, as I realized later still, was just the first stage of a much longer process.

I cried a lot. One evening Klaus put his arms around me and said, 'Poor duck, you copped it.' Tears sprang to my eyes. 'Oh, don't make me cry,' I said. 'Why not?' he asked, and held me as I did. It was so good, so comforting to be able to do that, to lean on his strength, cry on his shoulder when I needed to, and be held, and know that I didn't have to pretend to him or 'be strong' for him, or protect him. My tears never upset him. He knew what I was going through and he knew how I felt, and it didn't frighten him, he was just there with me, all the way through.

Toward the end of January I wrote to Karen in America, telling her of my surprise when the fears I hadn't known were there began to surface.

> Now that the body's recovery is just about complete, I'm beginning to let in the shock on all the other levels, and that will take longer to absorb. I think the mind throws up a protective barrier in a situation like this, so that we're given one thing to deal with at a time. I know the physical recovery would have been made far more difficult had I had to deal with all the rest of it at the same time. As it was, I was on a high for weeks – and although I felt a lot of sadness and did all the crying I needed to do, I didn't feel a single fear. But now all that's coming through – I suppose it would be strange if it didn't!

She wrote back immediately:

> What you say resonates with all I have experienced in grieving situations – first getting caught up on a high from the relief at thinking that you're coping grandly with the immensity of it, and then little by little life feeding it back to you in bits you can really deal with.

I needed a great deal of time to begin to deal with all the bits life was feeding back to me – time to be quiet and introspective, time to let myself down into sadness and fear, time to cry, to be as emotional, as thoughtful, as contemplative, as I needed to be, before I was ready to look outward and start picking up the threads again. That period lasted all winter, and when it drew to a close I realized that it had really been a period of retreat, of hibernation, of sitting still and paying close attention to myself, of slowly and steadily regaining my mental and emotional, as well as my physical, balance.

I now know that the process consists of many stages: as soon as you've finished with one, there is another to be gone through. It's like peeling an onion: layer after layer awaits you, each revealing the next. But in the first few months after diagnosis and surgery I declared at the end of each stage, 'There, that's it, I've done it.' It wasn't a question of 'getting back to normal'. That was never an objective for me; I knew life was going to be different, I didn't know what 'normal' was, and as for going back, I knew that wherever I was going, it wasn't back. But I more than once mistook the end of a stage and the transition between it and the next, for the completion of the whole process.

During that first stage – of shock-absorbing, and admitting to consciousness the first glimmers of the full significance of what had happened to me – I was more self-absorbed than I have been at any time in my life since adolescence. Cancer and all its issues, especially the possibilities of recurrence, a shortened life span and early death, preoccupied me to the exclusion of almost everything else. I had to give them my full attention, had to keep my eye and my thought trained on them, and I didn't need or want any distractions. There was no room in my consciousness for anything else.

Friends came to see me. I was glad to see them all, but was fully at ease only with the ones who met my need to talk about what was preoccupying me. I was taken aback when anyone failed to realize this and tried to 'take my mind off it'. Vexation bordering on paranoia arose if, after polite inquiries after my health, the person turned the conversation too quickly to some other topic. Until I had talked for a while about myself and what was happening to me, I had no other topics.

A person's own fears of cancer and death – and in the case of breast cancer, a woman's horror at the loss of a breast – may be triggered by what has happened to us. This may render it almost intolerable for them to be with us, or listen to us, even when they care and want to help. Some cannot handle it at all, and keep away from us altogether: understanding this will help protect us from unreasonable expectations and disappointment. Others come to see us, but are squeamish about what has happened to us and can't talk about it; they try to distract us and 'cheer us up'. I soon realized this, and was able to make allowances for it, but for the first few weeks of my convalescence my need to talk and be listened to was insistent, and my reactions sometimes rather extreme.

Shortly before Christmas an old friend came to visit.

Friday 24 December
E was here on Wednesday. There was something in her visit that I must learn from. She did not really want to talk about me, apart from the concerned questions she asked on arrival: I could see that. That is difficult for me, because I need to talk, and that need is still pretty undiscriminating. When someone clearly doesn't want to know, I feel that the most important part of me is being ignored. I don't want to be amused, or to have my mind 'taken off it'. It's not that I don't want to talk about anything else, or that I can't. But if I feel that *that* topic, my topic, is forbidden, it constricts me, it bothers me, it makes me feel rejected – no, not 'rejected', but somehow passed over, disregarded.

Anyway, this is what happened. E was enthusing about how well I looked, the picture of health, etc, and said 'You don't look any different.' And I laughed and said 'Oh, come on: look at me!' and glanced down at my front. I've got so used to people taking my one-breastedness in their stride that I was thrown by her reaction. She looked away, and said 'I can't. I'm squeamish.'

I realized I'd been inconsiderate, but I was still taken aback. I thought of Kate, and of how she had said, looking straight at my newly flat side on coming into my room in hospital, 'That's all right: why can't everyone do that, why do women feel they have to wear falsies? What's wrong with having one breast?' That spoiled me for anything else. It's what I feel, and I want everyone to feel it. But maybe not everyone will.

When I saw E next, a few weeks later, she spoke to me of her own fear of death, a fear that wakes her in the night, and we were able really to talk about it. Then I understood. The experience showed me that I needed to be more discerning, more rational and tolerant in my expectations of people, and more accepting of their fears.

By early January I felt so well that I started to indulge fantasies about going back to teaching at the start of my winter term on the 18th. Luckily, everyone whose advice I valued – Swamiji, Klaus, and the students who were looking after my classes – told me not to be silly, not to rush. Luckily, I had the sense to listen to them.

It was much too soon, and I really knew it. As soon as I started teaching, my energies would be directed outwards, my full attention focused on my students and their problems. Before I could do that, I had to work through my own problems. Once I was teaching I would no longer be able to attend fully to the process I was going through, and it would be short-circuited. The process had to be completed, or at least brought to a certain stage, before I could return my attention to teaching. It was essential that I allow it time and the space to unfold, for as long as it took to do whatever it was that needed to be done.

I had only a vague idea of what that was, and occasionally I used the word 'vegetating' to describe what I felt I was doing during much of that time. When people raised their eyebrows, I explained that I didn't mean I was being lazy, I was just waiting, to see what would grow.

Clare, who came several times to give me massage, knew exactly what I meant, and brought out a wonderful simile from her experience of growing vegetables. She told me how, when you planted a new seed, you had no idea how it was going to grow or what colour or shape or height it was going to be or what harvest it would yield; you just looked on, and watched it come up and develop, and it was always a surprise and delight.

I waited and watched to see what would grow.

Koye, who was teaching my Tuesday class with Clare, sent me a card with Ben Okri's poem, *African Elegy*. Two lines leapt out, and over the next few months they became a touchstone for me.

There are secret miracles at work
that only Time will bring forth.[9]

I sensed that this was what was happening during that time of vegetation, and these lines helped me to see that I had to give myself the space to let it happen; not to close it off by setting a date for my return to teaching, but to be quiet, and wait, and allow time to do its work. I asked Koye and Clare and the rest of the team to carry on teaching while I continued to vegetate – sometimes I thought of it as hibernating, sometimes as being on retreat, sometimes as just waiting – for another three months.

Healing takes time, and we should give ourselves that time if we possibly can, and not feel guilty about it. I would dearly love to think that all women with breast cancer, and their partners (and indeed everyone, woman or man, who has any sort of life-changing illness) could allow themselves the necessary time for the healing process to work, and for the journey within. This requires our full attention, for quite a long time.

Breast cancer doesn't happen just to the women who develop it. It happens to our partners and families and friends; everyone close to us is riding the roller-coaster with us. The most helpful thing anyone can do is to understand our need for healing time, and encourage us to take it. Klaus helped me in every way, but the most important thing he did for me was to see that it would be a long process and to let me go through it in my own time and my own way. Not once did he give me the feeling that *he* was in a hurry for me to 'be all right' or to 'get back to normal'. He simply accepted me as I was, and our situation as it was, and waited with me while the process unfolded.

I have always felt that what was happening was harder for Klaus than it was for me. He wouldn't have this ('I'm not the one who has to go to hospital and be cut,' he said), but I really do think that to stand by while someone you love suffers, and not be able to prevent it, must be harder than going through it yourself. I know it would be for me. In the early days, a great deal of my grief and anger were for him; it was unbearable to me that I might die and leave him alone.

And here was a fundamental change. I had always assumed that Klaus would die before me (he is 12 years older) and for as long as I can remember I've dreaded the prospect of his death, of having to continue my life without him. Sometimes, I had wished that I might go first. But the sudden knowledge that I might really die before him changed all that. I knew that that was *not* what I wished, that I didn't want to go first, that I didn't want him to be left alone, that I wanted to live, to be with him when he died, and see him through. I knew this in the same determining moment of answered prayer I've described earlier. It came out of the strength I had been given on that memorable night, and my trust in it: I knew, and I know, that I will not be given anything to bear that is beyond my capacity to bear it.

At the beginning of March I felt the first urge to sniff the air outside my burrow and dip into the stream of life again. On impulse I decided to go to Loutro, in southwest Crete, for a week in early April. Klaus and I had had two good holidays there; thinking about it, I longed to be there, to get up into the mountains and plunge into the sea.

On the plane, over the toe of Italy, I wrote:

Tuesday 29 March
The interesting thing about this journey is that at no time have I felt any apprehension, any anxiety. I always used to when going away on my own, leaving Klaus. Of course, the fact that 'I know the way' has something to do with it, but it goes deeper. What, after all, can there possibly be to be afraid of? And I realize now that I have been really very calm, very peaceful, for quite a while.

I have confronted death, come face to face with it. Now that passage from the *Isha Upanishad* has a new, deeper meaning:

Who sees all beings in his own Self, and his own Self in all beings, loses all fear.

We all die. Once we know we are no exception to that rule, we can, truly, 'see ourselves in all beings', truly share that common lot, that knowledge. And lose all fear.

Through Freelance Holidays I had booked a flower-walking holiday led by Jeff Collman, a professional botanist. I had wanted to do some 'serious' walking in the mountains above Loutro since we first went there, but Klaus wasn't keen, and I wasn't prepared to venture alone into those virtually uninhabited hills, where it's so easy to lose yourself or break an ankle miles from anywhere. I had only done short forays of an hour or so out of the village; here was my chance to go further.

'Walking with the Spring Flowers' sounds like a pleasant amble, but most of the walks were all-day expeditions that took us high into the steep, stony hills, and were a real test of stamina and fitness. Only four months after major surgery, I was up to it; the rucksack straps never even chafed my scar.

The walks were terrific. The April sky was clear, the air pure and crisp, the flowers beautiful – fields-full and hillsides-full of deep, rich, brilliant poppies and anemones and other, rarer plants whose names I never learned. Jeff was knowledgeable about them, and I enjoyed seeing them, but I was intoxicated with my real love, the wild, bare, majestic landscape of southern Crete, and after a brief inspection of what was going on at ground level I let my fellow-botanists get on with it while I looked up at the magnificent mountains.

I swam, too, whenever I got the chance, which was often several times a day: early in the morning before we set off, in the evening when we returned, and during the day whenever our route took us down to the sea. My father taught me to swim when I was five. I loved swimming then because he loved it, and I've loved it ever since. In fact, I love water – drinking it, bathing or showering in it, swimming in it, walking in the rain. Nothing wakes me up or cheers me up quicker than getting wet. Especially in the sea. That first moment of immersion is special, almost holy. After a swim in the sea I always feel refreshed, energized, revitalized. In southwest Crete the water is particularly clear and clean and lively, sparkling in the sun, reflecting every shade of blue from the sky. It's full of life force, and being in it is cleansing, life-enhancing.

Loutro lies at the foot of Crete's White Mountains, the Lefka Ori; the spring snow-melt flows into the Libyan sea and cold springs bubble up from the sea bed. The water is cold even in mid-June; at the beginning of April it was freezing. I got in quickly, submerged myself completely, and, as I've always done, pulled the straps of my swimming costume down to get as much of me as possible in contact with the water, baring my breasts – now my breast – to the sea. The cold salt water bathed my wound, flowed glacially over it, stimulating and cleansing and healing; within two minutes the icy cold was bearable and I would swim until it was time to get on with the walking.

A passage from the *Rig Veda* came into my thoughts often as I swam:

> *In the midst of the Waters is moving the Lord, surveying men's truth and men's lies. How sweet are the Waters, crystal clear and cleansing! Now may these great divine Waters quicken me!*

Wednesday 30 March
The last time I was here, nine months ago, I still had two breasts. Now, as I swim, I can see only one. I still slip my straps off as soon as I'm in the water. The view is different now. One breast hangs down, as I look down: the left side is flat, no breast there. It feels strange. In fact, to be here, so different, so soon after I was last here, throws everything into sharp relief. Of course, the tumour was there last June, unknown to me.

Wednesday 6 April

One thing this week has done for me is to make me feel 'normal' again. I've forgotten about cancer. Being one-breasted has been all right. It was a good week for me in every way. It was good to push myself physically. It was good to cope with being single-breasted in a group of strangers. It was good to travel on my own, with no anxiety. It was good to be welcomed in Loutro by Rob and Bob and Alison and Maria and the others – it was like coming home.

Duncan said, just after I got home from hospital, 'Do what gives you joy.' Crete, being in Crete, gives me joy. Swimming at Loutro, Marmara, Sweetwater, gives me joy. 'Walking' in the mountains gives me joy. Teaching gives me joy. Going for a walk in the park with Klaus gives me joy.

Peter said: Never postpone happiness.

On our second walk, high up in the Anopoli valley, Esje noticed a tree, stopped, and exclaimed to her husband, '*Peter – are there really buds on that tree?*' Its trunk was dead and gone, no wood, only a big swirl of grey bark left. Most of its branches were dead. But everywhere there were buds, about to burst into flower. Another metaphor. What an effort, what an achievement, what faith. However ravaged the body, we can still put forth buds, we go on flowering.

One of my favourite swimming places in Crete is Marmara Beach, a tiny pebble cove a couple of miles west of Loutro, with water even clearer and livelier. Marmara means 'marble': all the surrounding rocks are white marble, and there is a series of marble caves along the coast next to the beach. Most of them have only one entrance, but I had discovered two summers before that there was one I could swim into through one opening, turn a narrow corner where the sea swirled against the rocks, and swim out through another opening. It was dark inside, and somewhat scary, but exhilarating, and since that first cave swim it had had a deep significance for me – it was a metaphor for going through things and coming out on the other side. On our first day we ended up at Marmara late in the afternoon and I swam into my cave. Now my metaphor held a new meaning.

Saturday 16 April

Going to Loutro was the best thing I could have done. Apart from being a lovely holiday it showed me that I am well, that I am fit, that I can cope. The difference between now and January, just three months, is enormous. It took those months, every minute of them, to do the work that had to be done. And I've done it. If I haven't dealt with everything, I've at least reached a stage where I feel secure in the knowledge I have been given thus far, secure in myself, strong with my 'new' kind of strength. *That* knowledge, of where my strength comes from, has been with me ever since it first dawned, and it has never changed.

That's why I've never felt that I've been doing battle with cancer. I've lived with it and let it teach me. I've gone through it. And here I am, out the other side of the cave. There may be a long way to swim yet, but this I've done: I've swum into the cave, into the darkness, turned the corner, and swum out the other side, into the light.

And the tree, the blighted trunk with buds that Esje saw. The other metaphor of the week. How we go on, with faith, with confidence, doing what it is in our nature to do, doing what we were put here to do: creating, expanding, *living*, and we go on doing it until we die, however ravaged the body.

The week was a watershed. It marked the end of my retreat and the beginning of my return to life and work. I had decided to start teaching after Easter; returning from Loutro, I knew I was ready.

Saturday 16 April (continued)
I wonder how it will be. I feel as though I'm going out into the world, and that I'll be testing myself, watching myself to see 'how I am' once I get back into teaching. Will all the differences, all the secret miracles, be apparent in that context; will I operate differently?

Most of all, what I want for my return, is to just be myself, be relaxed, be glad to be there. I want whatever I am now, whatever I have become through this experience, to come through, to come up fresh. Not to fall back into old ways. Some 'old ways' may still be appropriate: I wasn't exactly a failure as a teacher. But I do want it to be new, to be fresh, to come from within me as I am now, not as I was then.

Those who are healed become instruments of healing
Swami Sivananda Radha

I had always known that the experience of cancer was going to be transformative, and that as long as I was able to use it creatively and learn its lessons, I would be a better teacher once I had come through it. Swamiji had reminded me to look forward, not back; to think of how my experience would, in time, help others. She had said 'All that matters is how you *use* the experience.' Knowing that its fruits, whatever they were, were going to come through in my teaching and benefit my students, was an exciting prospect; it helped pulled me through convalescence and recovery quickly, and was a key factor in my healing. It wasn't only for myself that I was going through cancer.

I thought, often, of Swami Radha's words. Years earlier, in a time of different difficulty, they had thrown a beam of light on my path; now, in the context of my healing from cancer their truth went deeper. If we understand illness not as an affliction but as a process of transformation, not as a calamity but as a teacher, and if we open ourselves to its teaching, whatever we become through it will be of use to everyone with whom we come in contact. It will flow back into the stream of life and contribute to the healing of the planet. Once the alchemy of illness has done its work, once we go through it and emerge, healed, on the other side, we will truly have become instruments of healing.

Sitting there in front of my students on Monday 18 April, ready to start my first lesson after five months away, I had no idea how my voice would sound or what words would come out. And everything did come up fresh, as I had hoped it would. My voice was softer, surer, and a tendency I had always noticed and disliked, to belabour points, to say too much, had gone. I was able now to say what needed to be said, and leave it to the students to make what they would of it; I seemed to understand better that while teaching was my responsibility, learning was theirs.

My students noticed the changes in my teaching. The most frequent observations were that there was 'more of me' now, which was exactly what I felt myself, and that there was more conviction in my teaching. It all comes down to my scribble on the plane to Crete: what, after all, can there possibly be to be afraid of now? Nothing: and freedom from fear has been the source of that deeper conviction. It has given me a surer voice.

The five months I spent waiting for time to bring forth the secret miracles that I knew were at work within me were healing time, a time of going through a profound process of growth and change, and in many ways they were the most rewarding months of my life.

I spent a great deal of time, probably most of my time, writing my journal. It became necessary, indispensable to me, as a tool for processing the experience of cancer. Writing helped me to look, to focus on whatever feelings and thoughts arose, to observe them and work with them.

It was therapeutic, of course, but it was more than that: it became a meditation practice. It gave me another means of drawing out for inspection everything that I needed to look at, which is exactly what meditation does, or should do. In the focused openness of meditation, or of writing, feelings and thoughts are given the space to rise into consciousness. When they do, in writing as in meditation I am *there*, wholly present, and can look at what arises.

This attentive self-observation encourages healing, for when the feelings that come with an experience have been drawn out of the darkness, when we have looked at them, accepted them, and integrated them into our consciousness, healing takes place.

Intuition had told me from the beginning that the most important thing for me to do on this roller-coaster ride was to stay in touch with what was happening to me and with how I felt about it, to be truthful about it and not to let any of it get lost. Thanks to the journal nothing did get lost. Whenever anything cropped up – a new fear, a new idea, an issue I needed to think through, a dream, a vague discomfort that I couldn't quite identify – I switched on the Mac and started writing.

Monday 27 June
Writing in this journal has become a habit, a truly helpful habit. There have been times when I've begun, started 'just writing', with nothing to say and nothing coming. But mostly my flying fingers, if I just let them go, seem to touch whatever is going on inside and draw it out for me to examine. It can't really be my fingers. It's my mind: when I write in my journal, it starts to focus on whatever is going on inside. It's a bit like focusing a camera (manual focus). At first everything is unclear, blurred, subterranean; one's vision swims, one can't see anything. Then, as one carefully turns the lens, the subject comes slowly into focus.

Often, I haven't a clue what it is that needs to be focused on, what it is that's going on inside before I start, but something always rises to the surface and becomes clear to me as I go on. Once it does, I can draw it out and look at it, give it a name, recognize it for what it is, and then it can never recede, fade, disappear, be buried, as it would do if I hadn't written it. Once it's out in the open I can look at it and I do look at it. And once I've really looked at it, the bonds loosen, and that's what it's all about. Little by little, I let go.

Once something has been pulled out of the murky unclear darkness into the clear light of day, it is there. It cannot slip back. No effort of will could re-repress it! Once it's out, there's no way I can avoid looking at it, and once it is looked at it can be assimilated, integrated into consciousness. Writing is helping me understand this process.

Everyone who gets cancer is exhorted to 'think positively', to maintain a 'positive attitude'. This is all very well as long as it doesn't lead us to deny our fears and our sadness, our so-called 'negative' feelings. I think that a genuinely positive (although I would rather call it a realistic) attitude allows us to let *all* of our feelings in and accept them as they are, whatever they are. This is what will free us, in time, from their hold over us.

'Being positive' can all too often mean avoiding reality (as when I balked at acknowledging my newly-surfacing fears because I thought of fear as 'negative', a bad sign). But reality is neither positive nor negative; it is simply reality. It is as it is. Being *too* positive can cut us off from the full spectrum of our feelings and mask our underlying fear of death, which is the very thing that has to be faced.

This is a tall order. To do it we may need help in integrating the enormity of the experience of cancer, and all its implications, including death, into consciousness; help in living with cancer, living with the knowledge of death. For some, individual or group therapy or counselling may be appropriate. Others may find the help they need in a cancer support group. Some may be fortunate, as I have been, in getting real spiritual help from their partners and friends; but because we often try, even unconsciously, to protect our loved ones from the full force of our feelings, it may be better and more helpful to talk to a qualified therapist or counsellor who is not personally involved.

(We need to find one, though, who can accompany us as we look at our deepest feelings without needing to reassure us; one whose own fears have been acknowledged so that they don't block our exploration of ours.)

But anyone who is going to look at the entire experience of cancer and get to the heart of its meaning, whether alone, or within a network of friendship and support, or in therapy, would, I think, find journal-keeping a real help. It's tempting, and it's easy, to bury our fears and sadness, our anger and despair, especially when, after treatment is finished, we get back into our life and have less time to contemplate. Journal-keeping helps ensure that we don't bury them.

I once came across a definition of depression that struck me as remarkably acute: *Depression is knowledge withheld*. When we withhold knowledge from ourselves, when we bury our feelings beneath the surface, when we avoid looking at our feelings about having cancer, about having lost a part of our body, about our changing lives and relationships, about our uncertain future, about death, we may become depressed.

Allowing our feelings to bubble up into awareness brings pain, of course, but it is the cleansing pain of awakening consciousness, rather than the dull, dispiriting ache of self-deception. It is the healing pain that will uproot the underlying depleting pain, the depression, and clear it away. Once we look at our feelings, once we acknowledge them, accept them, and take responsibility for them, they lose their grip on us, and we can let them go.

I had kept a journal sporadically all my life, but until I had cancer I had never done so consistently over any period of time. How did I know that this was what I needed to do? I don't know, but an inner voice said 'Do this,' and I did it. I remember the moment: I was in the shower on the morning of Thursday 4 November when that voice spoke from within. 'Start a journal,' it said. 'You are going on a roller-coaster ride, you are going where you have never been before, things are going to happen that have never happened before, it is going to be devastating, you are going to feel a lot of things. You are going to need to keep track of them. Write everything down. Record it, don't lose it. Some day it may be of help to others.'

That afternoon I opened a new file on my computer, and began.

I considered writing by hand, but events and my reflections on them were piling in so fast that my handwriting couldn't possibly have kept up with them. My fingers on the keyboard could, just about. But the important thing is to do it, to write and write and keep writing, even when what we are writing makes no apparent sense; write until what we are really feeling becomes clear to us, until we have drawn it out of ourselves and looked at it.

In *Peace, Love and Healing* Bernie Siegel describes a study in which 25 adults were asked to write down details of disturbing life experiences and describe their feelings about them:

> *A control group of equal size wrote only about superficial topics. Blood tests showed strikingly improved immune function among the emoters, who also made fewer visits to the doctor, but no improvements among the control group. Six months after the experiment was over, the emoters still showed positive health effects.*
>
> *By focusing on events that most people try to forget as quickly as possible, the emoters allowed themselves to express their feelings and hence gave their bodies 'live' messages. I also believe that the act of writing these events down allowed the emoters to rethink them. In other words, they engaged in a simple form of cognitive retraining. The events themselves remained the same but lost their destructive power.* [10]

Journal-writing helps us to free ourselves from the destructive power of painful experiences and our buried feelings about them. It helps us to remember, and to tell ourselves the truth. It helps us to know ourselves, to accept ourselves and our feelings, and to find our way through them to healing.

It helps Time to bring forth the secret miracles at work within us.

6 A Visible Wound

> Prosthesis offers the empty comfort of 'nobody will
> know the difference'. But it is that very difference I
> wish to affirm, because I have lived it, and survived it,
> and I wish to share that strength with other women.

Audre Lorde – *The Cancer Journals*

Towards the end of February an unexpected secret miracle began to
emerge. I started to notice an increasing reluctance to wear my
prosthesis.

I had never questioned that I would need a prosthesis for teaching
if for nothing else. So I had gone to a great deal of trouble to find
exactly the right one. I visited Breast Cancer Care (then the Breast
Care and Mastectomy Association), who offer a fitting service, and
spent two hours with Jackie, a cheerful, patient lady who sorted me
out, first with the perfect bra, and then with the perfect falsie. Then
I had a small skirmish with the Surgical Appliances Department at
the hospital: they didn't stock the model Jackie and I had settled on
and at first declined, but after much persuasion agreed, to order it
specially. Then there was a long search through the big London
stores for the bras: they had been discontinued and had to be ordered
from the manufacturer. When they finally arrived they had be sent
away to have special falsie-holding pockets sewn in. This all took a
couple of months. The experience showed me, somewhat to my
surprise, that having to wear a bra – I had discarded my last one
about thirty years earlier – might not after all be such a nuisance,
and that the prosthesis didn't feel cold and clammy and
uncomfortable as I had expected: in fact, once it was in place, I
scarcely noticed it.

When everything was finally ready I brought home bra and
prosthesis and proudly demonstrated them for Klaus, who took a long

thoughtful look at the newly two-breasted me and said, 'That's very nice, but do you really need it?'

Did I? It was three months since the mastectomy, and I had by now accepted my changed body. Through exercise and massage and loving attention I had reclaimed the operated area. I had accepted my scar, nine inches long, running diagonally from the base of my sternum into my left armpit; I had even come to like it, and to appreciate the firm, pristine hardness of 'my flat side'. I wasn't self-conscious; even at that early stage, going one-breasted into company wasn't a problem for me. Nevertheless, the answer I gave Klaus was the one that had felt right to me at the beginning: that although I might not need it for anything else, I certainly needed it for teaching; that it was unfair to inflict my changed appearance on my students, especially on my new students; that it was their class and they shouldn't be asked to deal with the evidence of my surgery, shouldn't be asked to look at a teacher with a missing breast.

But it was an old answer, an automatic answer, and I had moved a long way on from the state of mind I had been in when I first thought about it. Klaus had asked the question, and I now began to wonder whether there wasn't a new answer to it, whether it might not be possible for me to do without the prosthesis, whether I couldn't, after all, stand up in front of my students as I am.

The more I thought about it, the more I realized that I had become decidedly uneasy about sticking a bit of silicone gel on my chest to make myself look like something I'm not, to make it look as though I have two breasts when I don't. It felt like a concealment. Gradually I grew sure that wearing the prosthesis would not be right for my students any more than for me, that going in for such a pretence would undermine everything I try to encourage in my teaching: self-acceptance, compassion for others and oneself, acceptance of one's limitations and imperfections and those of others, acceptance of what *is*, of things as they are; willingness to be in the moment, willingness to move towards one's inner truth.

My reluctance to 'inflict' the sight of my flat side on my students gave way to the certainty that it was absurd to pretend to them that I was anything other than what I am. I had by then fully accepted my body as it was, and felt that I could trust them to accept it too.

Driving home from Harlow after one of Swamiji's workshops at the end of February, I told Annie and Tania how my thoughts were developing, and asked them for their views. Tania said that any difficulties in that situation would come from the woman herself: her self-consciousness, her discomfort, would call attention to itself and the missing breast, and that would make others uncomfortable too. 'You're comfortable with yourself,' she said 'so others are too – and besides, it really doesn't notice.'

Annie simply said, quietly, 'I think you should be as you are.'

That evening I spoke to Swamiji. She probed a little, to ascertain that I really did feel comfortable with myself, and that I could stand up in front of a class without being self-conscious. Then she said, 'Do it. You won't be inflicting anything on anyone. On the contrary, it will help people to see how you're dealing with it, to see that it's possible to cope with cancer without hiding.'

Making the decision freed me to think about the whole issue, and over the next few weeks I explored every aspect of it in the journal.

Monday 28 February

The first thing that struck me, last night, was that all my worry about 'new students' was misplaced, because some of them are of course going to become old students. In a few years I will be as close to them as I am now to the teacher-training group. How could I present myself as a two-breasted person, when I'm not? When would the point of revelation come? How could I wear the prosthesis in the beginners' class and not in the other classes, or at teacher training, when at least some of these 'new students' are going to be moving into those groups. How could I be double-breasted on Thursday and single-breasted on Monday, Tuesday and Saturday? It doesn't make sense.

Talking to Clare today, other things came up. It struck me that wearing the prosthesis, sticking this silicone chicken breast onto my chest, would negate all the openness with which I've dealt with my cancer so far. It wouldn't fit, it wouldn't be right. She said that my not wearing a prosthesis would be a gift to my students, and I realized how important it was to do it that way, to be honest and open about it.

This is how I am now. And how I am now, all of it, is there to be used for the healing of others – if I am really to be the better teacher I hope to be.

After a while I began to consider the wound itself, and what it meant to me. This revealed some surprising aspects of myself, and some feelings about what had happened to me, of which I had been unaware.

Thursday 10 March

What came up this morning was my feelings about my breast, my missing breast. It struck me that there is perhaps more to it than I've been acknowledging, that there may be something deeper underlying my comfort with my new appearance, my acceptance of the loss, my sense of the reality of the whole thing. I do feel all those things, I do feel, simply, that this is how it is, 'this is how I am now'. But it's not really simple. There is more to it, there is something else. I'm conscious of something like a sense of pride, or accomplishment, of achievement, in having a visible wound.

Having written that, I found that I wanted to insert the words 'at last' before 'having'. *In at last having a visible wound.*

I remember when I first started to feel good about the scar, when I started massaging and really stretching it. No, even before that, even before it healed, I didn't mind it. I not only didn't mind it, I felt good about it. I remember feeling good about it right after surgery, good about that hard, flat, firm area under the bandage, and saying to Alan Stoker, 'It feels good, it feels like a good operation.' He said 'It's just a straightforward operation,' and I said 'But it feels good, it feels all right.'

So even then, way back then, I didn't mind, I accepted my wound. I never thought of it as a disfigurement (though Klaus did once say, sadly, while I was still in hospital, 'It's a terrible mutilation' and I nodded and felt sad too). And then there was that Thursday night sadness, a week after the operation, when I wept for quite a long time for my lost breast; but after that I accepted, and developed a real affection for the scar, the flatness, the hardness, the absent-ness of the breast.

My wound gives me permission to fail. It says 'I have had a devastating experience, a cataclysm. I have coped with it well, and am living my life to the full, looking forward to and expecting many more years of full and useful life. Losing the breast has made no difference to my life (though having cancer certainly has). But having only one breast gives me permission not to be perfect. It is the visible, the irrefutable evidence, that I am not perfect. And I don't have to be perfect.'

I can go easier on myself. I don't have to drive myself. My flat left side makes it plain to everyone who knows me now or will know me in future, that I'm not perfect. And it's all right. It's all right, for instance, to be a little heavier than I'd really like to be, as long as I eat well and stay healthy. I can accept not being slim. (At last. At nearly 59 it's about time.) I can relax, knowing that no one can expect too much of me. Knowing that I can say no. Knowing that I don't have to push myself beyond my limits, knowing I have limits and that it's all right to respect them. I can still do my best, but I can stop when I'm tired, and rest. I can acknowledge failure and forgive myself, knowing it isn't so terrible to fail.

Nothing is terrible. I've been through cancer and survived and thrived, I've been transformed. What could be terrible now?

My wound is like a medal, a decoration, concrete, tangible evidence, proof positive that I've been through a devastating experience and come out on the other side.

Maybe there is another reason why I don't want to cover it up, don't want to wear the falsie. I definitely don't want to, for the reasons I've been conscious of: that I don't want to appear to be something I'm not; that I don't want to negate all my openness about cancer up until now; that it may be a help to others, and not just women, but men, too, to know that a woman can have a mastectomy and not have to hide the evidence. All those things are true. But maybe there is something else. Maybe I want, not just to be truthful, but to show my wound, to make it visible. Perhaps this helps me to feel that 'it's all right not to be perfect'. Maybe I need for other people to know what has happened to me and not expect too much of me, for me to give myself permission not to be perfect. If I appeared to be 'perfect' (ie physically: double-breasted) the people who know would forget, and the people who don't know would never know.

I do think there is something in this, and I will let it bubble for a while. Of course I know the next step, psychologically, the right questions to ask. Did I 'need' to get breast cancer and have a mastectomy to give myself permission not to be perfect? Was that the only way? If so, why? And can I now find a way of acknowledging and accepting that I'm not perfect without 'needing' to get cancer again?

I wouldn't put that question to myself now. Nor would I suggest to any other sick person that they 'needed' their disease, that they 'created' it, brought it on themselves. Illness holds lessons for us, but nobody 'needs' an illness: that judgement implies, whether intentionally or not, that illness is to be regarded as retribution, as a punishment for (or the consequence of) failure or stupidity. I also think it indicates a self-satisfied superiority on the part of the 'well' person who delivers the judgement. But what I think *is* true for many people – certainly it has been true for me – is that illness has its 'perks', in the form of the permissions we may now be able to allow ourselves: to get off the treadmill for awhile, not to strive so hard, but to meet life more quietly and take it more easily, to recognize hitherto unacknowledged needs. Once we do, we may be able to find ways of meeting our needs without being ill.

Looking forward like this is healthier than looking back; taking full responsibility for ourselves and our lives and our health in the future is more useful, more productive, than castigating ourselves for what we did or didn't do in the past.

Illness challenges us to change, to examine and redirect our lives, to 'push the reset button' as Bernie Siegel says. If we accept the challenge, illness is transformed from a burden into an opportunity, from an obstacle into a stepping-stone to healing and a richer, fuller life. Eventually, it will also be a stepping-stone to death, which is a part of life. Having had cancer, I know now that illness can be a powerful spur to our spiritual evolvement if we choose to use it to that end.

For me, an important part of this evolvement has been a greater measure of self-acceptance. The discovery that I regarded my wound as evidence that I am not perfect, and experiencing this discovery as a welcome release, was an astonishing turning point for me: astonishing because I thought I had long ago accepted myself and given up trying to be perfect. Clearly I hadn't. But now, perhaps, I could.

That discovery was part of the surrender, the acceptance of life as it is, part of the letting go of effort that from the beginning had lain at the heart of my healing.

Working my way through my feelings about my lost breast, and about my body as it now was, was a painstaking, painful, fascinating process, which led me to the realization, the *knowledge*, that I really was 'all right' as I was; and that knowledge was liberating.

We need to learn to love ourselves as we are and allow ourselves to be who we are, with all our apparent imperfections. All my life, it seems, I had been trying to be perfect. Now, the clear, physical, visible evidence that I was not perfect had finally emancipated me from that struggle.

But there was still much work to do.

Thursday 10 March (continued)

Was I so angry with myself for not being perfect that I grew a tumour so that I could lose a breast so that I could allow myself not to be perfect? Does this have a bearing on the alacrity and ease with which I accepted the thought of a mastectomy? I said yes, instantly, and never changed my mind. Did I want, did I know that I needed, a visible wound, an unmistakeable piece of evidence that I had been through a battle, a trauma? Did I think a lumpectomy wouldn't fill the bill?

I wrote a little earlier about 'at last' having a visible wound. Does that mean, perhaps, that I've always felt 'wounded', but not so that anyone could see? Did I hide, pretend things were better than they really were, so that my wounds would not be noticed? Yes, I did do that. My 'perfection' involved the need and determination to make everyone think I was perfectly happy. And did I do that so well that I eventually grew a cancer that had to be removed so that I could bring my wound into the open, let it be seen?

Once I had absorbed the first shocks – Alan Thompson taking the lump seriously and Alan Stoker saying 'I'm suspicious about this one, I'm 90 per cent certain you'll need surgery' – I moved forward quickly. After Dr Lin's shakeup, I accepted the idea of a mastectomy; and when, two days later, it was put to me, I unhesitatingly accepted the reality. The reason I gave – that a mastectomy seemed to give me a better chance of life without more upheavals – was a true reason; but was there this reason, too, that if I had cancer, and if I had to have surgery, was I happier with major surgery, surgery that would leave me with a visible wound?

(That conjecture strikes me now as somewhat overwrought. In retrospect I am sure that if I had been offered conservative surgery with any confidence I'd have accepted it happily.)

Now I'm going out for a walk in Oxleas Woods!

Later. The words 'visible wound' have been going round in my head all day. Sitting on a fallen tree-trunk in the woods, I let my mind travel round them, and let myself recall, vividly, some of the less visible wounds of the past. Whatever happened, whatever wounds I sustained, I successfully hid them, got on top of my feelings so that they wouldn't show. I always presented myself as happy, balanced, stable, unruffled, on top of things, able to function, never in any danger of losing control or breaking down.

And the thought arose that the lump, the tumour, was an accumulation, a synthesis, a coming-to-a-head, a symbol, even, the representative, of all the hidden wounds. No hiding this one, this accumulation of pain: it formed a big lump which had to be excised, cleansed out. I thought of it as a cleansing, a physical cleansing, very early on.

And now that the cut has been made, the accumulation cleansed, the breast removed, I have – at last – a visible wound, a wound that can't be hidden, a wound I don't want to hide. So I wear it boldly, proudly: here is my visible wound, my badge of honour. Proof that I've been through something big, and triumphed; proof that I've experienced and survived real pain, real wounding. In appearing single-breasted, my wound visible, I am saying 'I'm glad to show myself as I am.' But I'm also saying 'I'm not afraid to show and share my pain.'

This morning, I began to wonder if abandoning the prosthesis, for the reasons I was beginning to understand, was an uncalled-for display, almost a flaunting of weakness. I wondered if it wouldn't actually be a more 'grown-up', more balanced, decision to wear the prosthesis. That would say 'I've been in pain, I've been wounded, but I don't need to display it. I'm normal, and I want and expect to be treated normally, not like someone with a disability.' That's it, a disability. I felt it was almost like flaunting a disability.

But no. It isn't. It *is* more honest, more as I want to be, to show myself as I am, and not hide behind a false breast. All this questioning of my motives hasn't shifted my mind back towards wearing the prosthesis. But it is certainly giving me a fuller, deeper knowledge of the wound and what it means, and of how I feel about myself. And I think that as long as I understand, and apply my understanding to help me let go, take it easier, not try so hard to be perfect, the knowledge will be useful knowledge, good knowledge.

Do I want people to feel sorry for me? No. But am I thinking – am I hoping – that no one will now be inclined to judge me harshly or expect too much of me because I've had cancer and a mastectomy and have only one breast?

Friday 11 March

Thinking back on those early days, I'm aware that in my quick acceptance of the mastectomy there was an element of showing that there really was something seriously wrong with me. That it was no joke, no false alarm, but real and grave. So that everyone would know I really did have something wrong. I know I felt some uneasiness, after telling everyone about my lump, but before the diagnosis, that if it turned out to be 'nothing', everyone might think I'd been making a big fuss about nothing.

That's extraordinary. Why was that? Was I afraid of being thought a fake, a fraud? How could I possibly have been, how could I have had so little trust, so little faith in my friends and students, how could I have thought they would have been anything but glad for me had the tumour not been cancer?

Something of the same sort reared its head at the end of January, when I was starting to feel physically strong enough to contemplate returning to teaching, and began to say to myself 'Everyone must be thinking "Why doesn't she get off her bottom and get on with it?"' No one could possibly have been thinking that, but there it was: I had to struggle with that one for quite a time.

I suppose that has always been a deep fear: that I would be thought a fraud. If I was ever sick as a child, which didn't happen often, I had to be really sick, completely wiped out, to feel it was all right even to mention it, let alone not go to school, and I used to hide any minor ailment, like a sore throat, so that no one would notice.

Cancer presented me with a major, irrefutable whopper of an illness, and the mastectomy with the evidence of it, the visible wound. Interesting, then, that I should have got one of the few kinds of cancer that does leave a visible wound, and not one of the internal ones. Look, it says: I'm not a fraud. This really happened to me. It gives me a sense of relief, of release, of having paid my dues.

And of triumph. My flatness is like a badge I wear proudly. Like the flatness of the Amazon archer-warriors, who had their breasts removed to improve their performance with bow and arrow, it's a mark of honour. Proof that I have suffered, that I have at last joined suffering humanity. Did I need to suffer? Or did I just need proof that I have suffered? I don't really understand this yet. But I do understand my relief, my sense of release, at knowing that I can't any longer be thought a fraud, a fake.

None of this negates the good, the positive side of going single-breasted into teaching. I have no doubts about the rightness of that, even if, as I am now more aware, there are other reasons for doing it. It is going to be helpful to people, now and in the future. And it is more honest.

I've quoted these long journal passages to convey some idea of how much there is to sift through in the process of recovering from mastectomy surgery and coming to terms with all that it means. Of course not everyone would go through it in the same way as I have, or have the same feelings, or come to the same conclusions. Not everyone is going to feel as I do about prosthesis, or about the meaning of the wound, and I am not suggesting that mine is the only 'right' decision. Everyone is different, and we all need to come to our own decisions. But we do need to go through the process of finding out how we feel and acknowledging it, if we are to come through to full healing. We need to work through all the tunnels of our feelings about having cancer and losing a breast, out into the open space, the freedom, to which acceptance of reality, seeing the thing as it is, provides the key.

Because people are so terrified of cancer, even of the very word *cancer*, a thick cloud of denial hangs over the disease. It is hard for many to say the word, even to hear it, without flinching or shuddering. Breast cancer evokes that shudder in a very particular way. If a mastectomy is performed it leaves a visible wound, not only for the woman herself but for everyone around her, to come to terms with.

That process of moving toward acceptance of one's changed body and psyche is a vital part of the healing process, but for many women – and their families and friends – it is short-circuited by what the American writer Audre Lorde has called 'the travesty of prosthesis'.

A woman who has lost a breast is not the same as she was before, and nothing can make her so. She knows this in her heart, but she needs time to assimilate that knowledge. Yet within a few days of surgery, before she has even had time to recover fully from the anaesthetic, before she has even looked at her wound, let alone begun to absorb the colossal shock she has sustained, she is given a 'softie' breast form to put inside her bra, to fill out the space left by her lost breast, to make her look more like she looked before. Between the amputation and the pretence, scarcely a breath. Then, before she leaves hospital, she is fitted for her permanent prosthesis.

The prosthesis made to simulate a missing breast, unlike the prosthesis made to replace an amputated limb, has no function other than to conceal: to hide a woman's changed reality, to make her 'look normal', as if outward appearance were all that mattered. Its role is cosmetic.

The surgeon who sends a woman to be fitted for a false breast before she has scarcely begun to surface from the surgery that has amputated her real one, and others who encourage her to believe that by wearing a prosthesis she can be 'just as she was before', are encouraging her at this highly critical time to hide her wound and push away her pain, rather than let it in, look at it and come to terms with it. They are setting her feet on the path of denial.

The breast is only a part of the loss. A woman who has breast cancer is facing other losses too – most bitterly, the possible loss of the long, full life she thought would be hers. She is experiencing the frightening loss of control over her life and over what is happening to her. She is facing the loss of time and opportunity to complete her work. In facing death she is facing the loss of her partner, her friends, her children; of everyone she loves and everything she values. But instead of being given help to take all this in, to acknowledge the trauma she has suffered and her feelings about it, and to look at the deeper implications of having cancer, the woman who has had breast surgery is encouraged to distance herself from her feelings, and to delude herself and others that the loss she has suffered is merely a cosmetic loss, to be made good by the application of a piece of silicone gel.

At a time when she is exceedingly sensitive and vulnerable, she is side-tracked: deflected from beginning the essential process of facing, accepting and dealing with the reality of what has befallen her. Longing to believe that she can be as she was before the nightmare began, she eagerly welcomes the suggestion, implicit in the very haste with which the prosthesis is offered, that this is possible. Reinforcing the determination she may be feeling to 'get back to normal', this can inhibit the vital process of coming to terms and even arrest it altogether.

I think this is tragic, and I think it has serious consequences for recovery and healing.

I don't say these things critically. My experience of having surgery and being cared for in an NHS hospital has given me great respect and admiration for the skill and dedication and compassion of doctors and nurses. Their intention, when they hasten to get a woman who has just lost a breast fitted for a prosthesis, is surely to be kind and helpful. But I am not at all sure that it is helpful at this stage.

This widely pursued course of action seems to me to be based on three questionable assumptions.

One is that it will help a woman 'get back to normal' as quickly as possible. But that isn't possible, or even, necessarily, desirable. Having cancer changes a person. It can be a unique opportunity for looking at one's life, for taking stock, for making healthy, beneficial changes, for spiritual growth, tranformation and healing. If that opportunity is to be taken, encouragement and help are needed not in 'going back', but in going forward into the new, changed, healed life. Any suggestion that 'back' is the right direction to go in may obstruct the movement forward. As for 'normal', whatever may have constituted normality before, that too is going to change.

Secondly, it is assumed that wearing a prosthesis will restore a woman's self-confidence and help her to avoid feelings of inadequacy and loss of femininity and sexual appeal. But because the implication is that she is not all right as she is, and must pretend to be otherwise by covering up her wound and making her new shape look as much as possible like her former one as quickly as possible, it must, surely, have the opposite effect.

The third assumption is that wearing a prosthesis is the only way for a woman to live life after a mastectomy, that there is no other option. But there is, and it is a valid option, and women should be given time and space to consider it, to realize that it may be all right to have, and to be seen to have, only one breast.

Given this time, a woman might decide that it isn't necessary for her to hide her wound. Her decision will depend on a variety of factors: her age, her relationships, her social life, her position at work, her family's feelings. If she eventually decides that she does want to wear a prosthesis she will by then have accepted herself as she is, and it will take its place in her life not as an instrument of concealment and denial, but as a useful, practical asset. She can wear it all the time, or leave it off some of the time. She isn't its prisoner; she is free to use it as she wishes.

And if she decides to do without a prosthesis, she can still wear one on the occasions when she wants to, or when it may feel inappropriate not to. The point is that time and reflection – the time she has taken to absorb the change that has taken place, and to reflect on the emotions it has unleashed – have given her the choice.

The decision was comparatively easy for me. I am fortunate in having no external constraints on my choices; in being self-employed and independent; in not having a career ladder to climb or a social life to worry about as a younger and/or single woman would; and in living amongst a circle of friends, colleagues and students who share my outlook and support my choices. Above all, I share my life with a man who was able to accept my single-breastedness (as he delightfully calls it) immediately and unreservedly, who accepts me now, as he has all through our 35 years together, as I am. Klaus's acceptance made my acceptance of myself much, much easier.

So I have to admit that we have had heated discussions about the prosthesis question! Klaus argues that the situation would be very different for women whose aspiring managing-director husbands need to entertain their way up the corporate ladder, or who are themselves aspiring managing directors, or for younger women of any profession, or for women whose husbands want to take them dancing or to Ascot or the dog races. He says I don't realize that most women's lives are different from mine, and that most women wouldn't feel themselves free (nor indeed would many of them be free) to make the decision I have made.

Of course all this is true. Wearing a prosthesis may be appropriate for many sound reasons, and I know that that will be most women's choice. I know that my decision is, and will perhaps always be, a minority decision. But I also know I am not unique. I feel sure there are women besides myself, who, given the time, given the opportunity, given the help and guidance, given the awareness of single-breastedness as a legitimate option, would let themselves be as they are. And part of being as you are is letting yourself be seen as you are – seen not only by others, but even more importantly by yourself, whenever you look in a mirror or down at your chest.

I hope it is clear from all I have said that I don't think wearing a prosthesis is 'wrong'. What I do think is that we should have time to make the choice. Of course the decision to wear a prosthesis is valid as long as it is a real decision, based on what feels right and authentic for the woman herself after working through the whole trauma of cancer and mastectomy. But it may not be valid – it may not even be a decision – if she is rushed into it to hide her 'deformity' before she has even begun to recover from surgery, or made to feel she 'ought' to in order to spare others the sight of her altered body, or if she is led to believe that it will be of any real help in absorbing the immense shock of what has happened to her.

It's often said, appropos of the ability of the modern prosthesis to simulate the shape and texture of a real breast, that once you have been properly fitted you will feel 'just as you did before' and that 'no one will know the difference'. You *will* know the difference, and you aren't going to be as you were before. That is not possible. But trying for it robs you of the chance to explore and accept your wound as it is, not as a deformity but rather as a difference, a change in the landscape of your body. It robs you of the chance to explore the reality of what has happened to you, and the possibilities for change and renewal and true healing that come through acceptance of things as they are.

A woman who senses the truth of this may feel strong enough to ask for her fitting to be deferred while she takes time to get acquainted with her new self. But people in hospital are generally disinclined to upset the routine, and most women who have just had major surgery will be in no state to question the standard procedure. Most will go along with it, quietly accepting the 'softie' and the quick referral to the Surgical Appliances department. It is up to those who are looking after them to consider whether the procedure is helpful.

Perhaps any surgeons, hospital doctors, nurses, physiotherapists, counsellors and support people who read this will reconsider the wisdom of immediate fitting. It might be more appropriate to discharge women with an appointment for a fitting two or three months later, or at least to offer that option. If a woman was herself eager to be fitted sooner she could ask for an earlier appointment. Many women, I think, would make good use of the time.

Some women choose to be reconstructed in preference to wearing an external prosthesis, and immediate reconstruction is offered by some hospitals at the time of mastectomy. Reconstruction is done in either of two ways: with a silicone implant, or using live tissue from the woman's abdomen or back. One involves having a foreign substance permanently in one's body (which may carry risks: silicone breast implants have been suspected of causing cancer elsewhere in the body); the other involves major surgery. Neither of these options would have been acceptable to me, though I can see that their outcome, a permanent false breast without the inconvenience of an external prosthesis, might be attractive to others.

Reconstruction should unquestionably be available to any woman who wants it, but I think that everything I've said about the immediate fitting of prosthesis applies also to immediate reconstruction, and that it is more helpful to leave a space after mastectomy before taking either step.

Toward the end of March, ready to emerge from hibernation and just before going off to Loutro, I gave a full day workshop for my students to celebrate the coming of Spring and my imminent return to teaching. Sue Opie came, bringing a present for me: a copy of *The Cancer Journals* by Audre Lorde. She had told me about it a few weeks earlier, and I had been looking out for a copy. I read it that night; it was a revelation. Here were further aspects of the prosthesis question, aspects I hadn't considered.

Audre Lorde, who died in 1992 after surviving breast cancer for 14 years, was an American, black, lesbian, feminist poet and teacher. *The Cancer Journals* is essential reading for any woman who has had breast cancer, and especially for anyone who is beginning to question the need for a prosthesis. Reading of her experience helped me to clarify my views.

> *After a mastectomy, for many women including myself, there is a feeling of wanting to go back, of not wanting to persevere through this experience to whatever enlightenment might be at the core of it. And it is this feeling, this nostalgia, which is encouraged by most of the post-surgical counselling for women with breast cancer. This regressive tie to the past is emphasized by the concentration upon breast cancer as a cosmetic problem, one which can be solved by a prosthetic pretence. The American Cancer Society's Reach for Recovery Programme, while doing a valuable service in contacting women immediately after surgery and letting them know they are not alone, nonetheless encourages this false and dangerous nostalgia in the mistaken belief that women are too weak to deal directly and courageously with the realities of our lives...*
>
> *To imply that a woman can, yes, she can be the 'same' as before surgery, with the skilful application of a little puff of lambswool and/or silicone gel, is to place an emphasis upon prosthesis which encourages her not to deal with herself as physically and emotionally real, even though altered and traumatized. This emphasis upon the cosmetic after surgery re-inforces this society's stereotype of women, that we are only what we look or appear, so this is the only aspect of our existence we need to address. Any woman who has had a breast removed because of cancer knows she does not feel the same. But we are allowed no psychic time or space to examine what our true feelings are, to make them our own. With quick cosmetic reassurance, we are told that our feelings are not important, our appearance is all, the sum total of self.*[11]

Audre sees the way women are hurried by surgeons and support agencies into wearing a prosthesis as a conspiracy to silence women and to trivialize breast cancer, to assign it the status of a cosmetic problem to be solved by a bit of silicone gel. She sees it as a conspiracy to disempower women by dividing them from their pain, from their reality, a conspiracy to define them solely according to their appearance. She believes this conspiracy is founded on an attitude towards women that regards them as objects of attraction, and the loss of a breast as a cosmetic issue that can be solved with a falsie. Its effect is that women who have experienced breast cancer and mastectomy are cut off from their experience, are given neither time nor encouragement to confront its real issues, or to acknowledge and come to terms with their real and profoundly painful feelings about them.

Whether it is a conspiracy or not, I am sure she is right about the effects on women of the emphasis on prosthesis and of the assumptions underlying that emphasis. But this feminist view of the issue is surely not the whole story. I suspect that at the root of it is denial: the denial of pain, the denial of the full trauma of cancer surgery, and above all the denial of death. At the heart of it is our fear of death and our refusal to acknowledge it; our unwillingness to share one another's pain, our helplessness when faced with the pain of others, our inability to deal with our own pain and above all with the inevitability, the reality, of our own eventual death.

Fear and denial of death are an intrinsic part of our Western life. For all kinds of reasons, not least the success of medical technology and skill at prolonging life and delaying death, we have come to dread death as life's antithesis, the ultimate failure. Doctors, whose training is geared toward the preservation of life, and for whom death is the supreme enemy to be conquered, are probably even more inclined to this view of life and death than the rest of us. The surgeon who removes a woman's breast and who knows that this isn't the whole story, who knows that cancer may recur and that this woman may die from it, has his own pain to deal with, and this cannot be easy for him. In appearing to regard such an amputation as a matter of changed appearance, reversible by silicone gel, he may not so much be denigrating the woman or trivializing her pain, as shutting off his own.

Getting to know Alan Stoker opened my eyes to the pain surgeons daily undergo. He is gentle, compassionate, a healer. He doesn't denigrate women or trivialize breast cancer or underestimate the trauma of mastecomy. Nor does he deny his own pain. Knowing him made me reflect on how distressing it must be for doctors to deal with cancer. Surely there are others as compassionate as he is who are unable to show their compassion because they are less able to accept and tolerate the pain. How strong the impulse must be, for such a doctor to push his pain aside.

And how easy, then, for him to encourage his patient to do the same with hers, to hide her wound, her pain, her reality, behind a false breast. Genuinely wanting her to 'be all right', he unthinkingly undermines the process by which real all-rightness, which grows out of self-exploration, self-knowledge, self-acceptance and acceptance of reality, comes about.

Friday 24 December
I wonder what it's like to be like him – to be facing this illness all the time, lopping people's breasts off and giving them their prognoses, and caring about them as he so obviously does. I can understand now why some surgeons appear – and can really get to be – hard, callous, unsympathetic. How must it be, even for an 'ordinary' surgeon, to be facing this all the time, getting to know people, getting to care about them, and knowing that some of them are going to die?

Perhaps it isn't surprising that they switch off, withhold their sympathy, behave towards patients as if they are numbers, statistics, carcases. But how remarkable to be like Alan Stoker: to do it, to face it, to do these operations, to get to know people, year in and year out, and to care, and keep on caring, and growing in compassion and wisdom and power and ability to help and to heal. How is it that with some people, the caring, the compassion, grows, doesn't shrivel or get blunted, but grows? And how much does it hurt, what is it like for him when someone has a recurrence, or dies?

I almost feel – yes I do feel – I couldn't do that to him. Well I won't!

The rush to fit the woman who has had a breast amputated with a prosthesis also reflects our society's attitude to so-called disfigurement or deformity (and probably also to disablement of any kind). The in-built assumption that such things are not pleasant for others to see, pushes the woman who has undergone mastectomy into appearing 'normal' in order to be socially acceptable.

But let us be clear about this: it is, mostly, women who are compelled to hide their deformities. In a memorable passage in *The Cancer Journals*, Audre Lorde refers to Moshe Dayan's missing eye:

> *When he stands up in front of Parliament or on TV with an eyepatch over his empty eye socket, nobody tells him to go get a glass eye, or that he is bad for the morale of the office. The world sees him as a warrior with an honourable wound, and a loss of a piece of himself which he has marked, and mourned, and moved beyond. And if you have trouble dealing with Moshe Dayan's empty eye socket, everybody recognizes that it is your problem to solve, not his.*[12]

What is also at work here is the pervasive and powerful tyranny of 'the Body Beautiful'. Fuelled by television, films, magazines and advertising as well as by overall social pressures, it gains its grip on us in our earliest childhood, and we are all – men as well as women – to a greater or lesser degree held captive by it. It persuades us that we are acceptable as beautiful, as desirable, as women, only if we have certain attributes, including two breasts.

Of course, both the idea and the reality of mastectomy cut to the heart of every woman's self-image and sense of her femininity, and every man's view of what is appealing and sexually attractive in a woman. But we have a choice. We can respond to the tyranny by wearing a false breast so that we appear to have two. Or we can respond by rejecting the tyranny, by realizing that it's all right, albeit different, to have only one.

Audre Lorde also raises the political issues that surround breast cancer, mastectomy and prosthesis. She believes that women who have had mastectomy surgery are railroaded into covering up their wounds by a society that does not want to know, and that the reason it does not want to know is that it is refusing to face the immense and horrifying implications of environmental and food pollution. This, I think, is absolutely true, and although the political issue did not directly influence my decision not to wear a prosthesis, which I had made before I began thinking about it, it has certainly given me another reason to be comfortable with it.

That decision arose from a deep distaste for concealment. I did not want to hide, or conceal the truth of what had happened to me from others or from myself. But quite soon, I realized that I also wanted not to collude in the conspiracy of denial and silence that surrounds breast cancer. I wanted to be visible.

My visibility asserts not only my wish to be truthful with myself and others about my own reality, but also my commitment to openness and honesty about breast cancer, to doing what I can to help other women who experience it, and to help stem the scourge. It is a statement. It is a personal statement, but it is also, inevitably, a political statement, because breast cancer is a political issue.

One in 12 women in Britain will develop breast cancer at some stage of her life. Our death rate from breast cancer is the highest in the world, and our five-year survival rate one of the lowest. In the United States the incidence is even higher − 1 in 10 − but the death rate is lower. Every year in Britain, 30,000 women are diagnosed with breast cancer and 15,000 die of it. This, as Dr Cathy Read points out in *Preventing Breast Cancer: The Politics of an Epidemic*, is equivalent to a jumbo jet crashing and killing everyone on board, every week of the year.

Although the risk increases with age, breast cancer is not exclusively an old woman's disease. It is the leading cause of death among young women aged 35-54. Three young students of mine had breast cancer in their late 20s or early 30s. The breast cancer epidemic should be a major issue on the political agenda, but it isn't, yet. Increased publicity and growing dismay over the worsening statistics have begun to ruffle the surface of the silence that shrouds it, but there is scant evidence that the political will needed to attack it is gathering.

But women are getting angry, and anger is beginning to be channelled into action. In the United States, where there were 182,000 new cases and 46,000 deaths in 1994, fury about breast cancer mobilized women and their families and friends into a concerted force for action, and in 1991 the US National Breast Cancer Coalition was formed. Cathy Read says:

> *Rage fuelled the activism which enabled women throughout the country to organize into a national coalition in 1991. It provided women with a direct line into Congress. In just three years the movement has achieved remarkable success; $43 million extra for breast cancer research in its first year and $300 million extra in the second, with the largest slice diverted from the army budget. Just as important, the women gained a say in how the money should be spent.*[13]

The American achievement has inspired a similar movement in Britain. The UK National Breast Cancer Coalition was formed in July

1995 by a representative group of breast cancer activists, MPs and organizations and charities concerned with breast cancer. The Coalition has begun its campaign for a national strategy to beat breast cancer on three fronts: access to state-of-the-art treatment for all women with breast cancer; higher priority for and significantly increased government spending on research into causes and prevention; and a full and influential role for women in decisions regarding all breast cancer issues.

The UK Coalition has its work cut out for it. In Britain, the level of spending on breast cancer research is ludicrous: less than £3 million in 1995 compared with a defence budget of £22 billion; this despite the appalling death rate from a disease which may prove – contrary to the view that has prevailed for many years – to be at least partly, and perhaps largely, preventable. We don't yet know: research has been sporadic and unco-ordinated and has concentrated on early detection and treatment; the right questions about causes and prevention are only now beginning to be asked. These have to do with the effects of widespread pollution of the environment with toxic chemicals; the effects of the pollution of food with carcinogenic agents in growing crops and packaging them, and the feeding of hormones to animals slaughtered for meat; the effects of hormonal medication such as the contraceptive pill and hormone replacement therapy; and with diet.

If scientists investigating these factors conclude that any or all of them are in fact implicated in causing breast cancer, considerable political resolve will be needed to act on their conclusions. Powerful interests subvert scientific research and the implementation of its findings: the multi-national industries that produce and sell chemicals, for example, have always resisted the efforts of governments to ban them. These vested interests influence our personal choices and behaviour too. Cathy Read notes that in 1992 the British government spent £55,000 promoting breast-feeding, which has long been accepted as healthiest for babies and is now thought to protect against breast cancer as well, while the baby-food industry spent £12 million promoting baby-food.

Sustained research into the causes of breast cancer and the political commitment to act on its findings in the long-term interests of prevention are clearly the priorities in my view, but funding for higher standards of treatment – better screening programmes, training of breast cancer specialists, and well-equipped, adequately staffed breast cancer units in regional hospitals – is also urgently needed.

Karel Sikora, Professor of Clinical Oncology at the Royal Postgraduate Medical School, Hammersmith, West London, and Joint Director of Cancer Services for the West London Cancer Centre, wrote in the November 1994 issue of *Reader's Digest* that although America has a much higher incidence of breast cancer, it has a much lower death rate. He attributed the difference to the fact that in America diagnosis and treatment are organized better.

In Britain, he said, surviving breast cancer is a lottery. One reason for this is the shortage of cancer specialists. In Britain we have 272 clinical oncologists each of whom sees 560 new patients a year (the recommended maximum is 350) and has up to 2,000 patients in his or her care. In the United States an oncologist sees 200 new patients a year and in Norway the figure is 75. Only 40 per cent of women diagnosed with breast cancer will see a specialist. At least half of all women diagnosed with breast cancer are treated by general surgeons who see far too few cases to build up the expertise required to treat the disease properly.

Professor Sikora went on to speak of the work of the West London Cancer Centre, formed by the merger of the oncology units of Hammersmith and Charing Cross hospitals, and of a proposed scheme for the setting up of 300 similar specialist cancer units in district general hospitals nationwide. He estimated that such a scheme, which could save 3,000 lives a year, would cost £100 million a year.

> *While both the Government and the Opposition are currently pledged to improve cancer care, my fear is that as soon as the next general election is over, the Treasury's cash box will be shut tight and we will revert to the piecemeal, with patients taking pot luck. This must not happen…*
> *It's time to give British women the standard of treatment other countries take for granted.*[14]

These are political issues, and their solutions must be found at the political level. Now that a clear demand from women is beginning to be made through the UK National Breast Cancer Coalition, the solutions may be nearer. We must hope that the British government will hear the demand, follow the Americans' lead, and release substantial funding for research and for improved standards of diagnosis and treatment.

But whether or not we want to take part in political action, I think that each of us who has had breast cancer has a personal decision to make about how we might be able to use our experience to help bring these solutions about.

In Britain, as in the United States, there live hundreds of thousands of women who have been treated for breast cancer and so far survived it. Yet it would seem that American women generally find it easier to share their experience, whereas in Britain the individual woman who develops the disease remains more likely to endure it in isolation, reluctant to tell anyone, wondering what she may have done to cause it, struggling with guilt and shame and confusion as well as with the illness itself, and hiding her pain.

But as long as so many of us remain isolated individuals, political change – which happens only when enough concerned individuals unite and demand it – will be slow in coming. A significant step towards effective action to end the scourge of breast cancer could be for those of us who have survived it to come out of the closet and, as Audre Lorde says, 'become visible to one another'.

Sometimes, when I find myself amongst large groups of people – in the park, on a railway station, in a museum – I look about me at the women. I see no one like me; everyone seems to have two breasts. I know the statistics, I know that at least some of the women I see around me have had the same experience, the same operation, as I have had – but where are they? For some time this question disturbed me profoundly.

Sunday 27 March
It's so sad, so painful, that people feel they have to hide their pain, to pretend it isn't there, that nothing happened, that they are 'just the same as they were before'. I know I mustn't judge, I know everyone has to find their own way through, but I know, too, that that way of dealing with it is not dealing with it. It's such a denial – not only of the pain, but of what life has to offer. It's a denial of the gifts and the blessings which every real, deep experience holds at its core, and which are revealed to us only if we open ourselves to the experience, turn towards it, welcome it.

Walking through Greenwich Park this afternoon I thought about the pain of the women, the thousands and thousands of women, who have had breast cancer. And I thought: there must be thousands of women who have had mastectomies, walking around wearing prostheses, hiding the evidence, hiding their pain, pretending for their own sakes or for the sake of others that they are 'just the same as they were before'. Out of misery and loneliness, or simply English reticence, not daring to share. Out of genuine reserve, shrinking from having to deal with other people's reactions. Out of misguided generosity, sparing others the 'horrible sight'. There are so many reasons why a woman might do it. But perhaps, if more help of the right kind were available, some women at least would be able to come to grips with their pain, and work through it to an acceptance of themselves as they are, and be able to stand before the world as one-breasted women.

Friday 22 April

And what of the men: the husbands, the lovers, the partners? Can they really want the women they share their lives with to pretend they have two breasts when they only have one? Isn't it a new shock, every night, when the chicken breast comes out of the bra and the flatness and the wound are exposed again? And how about the chicken breast itself? Do men want to see it lying flabbily around? Or are women content to pack it tidily away in the airing cupboard, content to keep it hidden?

Klaus's reaction to seeing and handling a prosthesis for the first time while I was in hospital was *ugh*. I am so grateful to him for accepting me so absolutely, so unquestioningly, for not only not making me feel I ought to wear a prosthesis, but gently, actively encouraging me not to. I know how to appreciate that properly now, for I know better now how important his acceptance has been for my growth, for my acceptance of myself, and how crucial to my decision to reject prosthesis. He knew me better than I knew myself, all along. He knew I wouldn't, couldn't do it. Whatever he felt about the wound, he accustomed himself to it. He accepted it as part of me. And although I know he regards it more as mutilation than I do, still it must be easier for him to be aware of it all the time than to see me all day long with 'two breasts', and then be hit anew with my flat side and my scar whenever I undress.

It would be good to talk to some men and find out what they feel about it. Perhaps some of them, or even most of them, would go along with whatever their partners wanted to

do, perhaps they would support and even encourage them to
be themselves, to go single-breasted. If women themselves
were given encouragement to be truthful, if the possibility,
the viability, of going without a falsie, were aired, if the whole
structure of treatment weren't based on the assumption that
all that mattered was 'getting back to normal'. That is
impossible. And all that is accomplished is that women's
anger, grief and terror, women's wounds, are swept under the
carpet so that others don't have to look at them.

I don't know what would have happened if I had had a quicker, easier
time of getting fitted for a prosthesis. But it was three months before I
was properly kitted out, and by then I had had time to grow
comfortable with my changed body, and knew that I didn't need or
want to hide the change. I am glad that circumstances gave me that
time. For me, the whole process of coming to terms with cancer would
have been more difficult and prolonged had I got the prosthesis sooner.

My visible wound is a constant reminder of what has happened to
me. On the practical day-to-day level it reminds me that I need to take
care of myself, eat properly, make sure I get plenty of time and space for
myself, and plenty of rest and deep relaxation. It reminds me of the
need to do all I can to avoid a recurrence of cancer. On the spiritual
level, cancer has deepened my knowledge of life and death, and of
myself. Out of it have come good changes, life-enhancing changes, and
I don't want to slip back into old patterns. I do not want to forget that
I have had breast cancer.

Within a year of my mastectomy I had grown completely used to
having only one breast. I feel comfortable with it, at ease with myself. I
am not conscious of being stared at, or of eyes being uneasily averted
when I am out and about. Before I returned to teaching, I expected to
feel a bit nervous and exposed at first, but when the day came I didn't,
and I never have. My students have taken it in their stride. I refer to it
occasionally so that they'll know that it isn't an 'unmentionable'; and I
know they would feel they could talk to me about it if they needed to.

Swamiji had said that by 'teaching as I am' I would be helping
people to see that it is possible to have cancer and to cope with it
without hiding. At the time I was simply grateful to her for affirming
the decision and giving it added weight, added rightness, but later I
came to see how significant that aspect of it was. On the first May
Bank Holiday, shortly after I returned to teaching, Clare came and
spent the day with me.

Wednesday 4 May
Clare and I talked at length in Oxleas Woods on Monday about prosthesis, and the whole issue of denial. She said, 'When you don't wear one, when you are honest about what has happened to you, you give a gift to thousands of people.' And, she said, 'it breaks the cycle of denial, of hiding.'

I had not seen that. But of course my deciding as I have, my acting as I have, must have more of an impact than a purely personal decision, a purely individual action. That decision, that action, that statement, made by any woman, would have ripples, would affect all her family and friends, and their families and friends, and so on. But my decision, my action, my statement, as a teacher of yoga, has wider ripples, reaches so many more people. I stand in front of some 70 students every week in my four classes, and the statement is conveyed not just to them but to all their families, all their friends.

It is important. And I'm glad I've chosen to do it. And that's yet another reason why I needed all the time I took. Had I returned earlier to teaching, it would have been with a falsie on my front.

I remember now, how, on Christmas Day, 1993, five weeks after my mastectomy, walking in Greenwich Park with Klaus, I suddenly felt a rush of joy, and I thought, 'I feel whole!' I looked down at my 'flat' side and said to myself 'This is how I am now. And it's all right.' Since then there has been much to deal with, much to come to terms with. And there is more to come: it won't be over until my life in this body is over. But that essential sense of wholeness, of having come through, of acceptance of things as they are, of being all right as I am, has never left me, and I trust it never will.

I hope that by being as I am, by teaching as I am, I am helping to break the cycle of denial and silence that surrounds breast cancer, the denial and silence that contribute so much to fear, and to the hiding of pain, and to the consequent isolation endured by so many women. And, I hope, making it a little easier for other women who experience breast cancer to accept themselves as they are and to move towards full healing.

7   A Glancing Blow

Sunday 20 March

Last Sunday, on the way to Harlow, I had an experience that I
called one of precognition. It was an extraordinary experience,
but so much happened after it that it got overlaid; I didn't think
about it again, and didn't write about it. But this morning Klaus,
having looked at the damage to the car for the first time,
commented on how strange it was. He said it looked burned,
melted. And so I started to think about it again.

This what happened last Sunday. As I was driving up the
M11, a large, black bird flew across and just above the path of
the car. The sight of it triggered a vision: an intense, fearful,
realistic vision of a large bird flying into the windscreen and
crashing through it into my face. It all flashed through my mind
in seconds; I *saw* it: myself and the car all covered in blood and
feathers and bits of broken bird; splinters of shattered
windscreen in my face, me closing my eyes against them and
risking a terrible accident, and, finally, driving off onto the hard
shoulder, unable to continue driving. What next crossed my
mind was 'It would be "better" (that was the word I used to
describe the alternative scenario I then imagined) if the bird
were to crash through the windscreen on the other side, the
empty, passenger side.'

I have never had a thought like that before. I know that
windscreens can shatter, but the prospect has never actively
worried me, and it has never occurred to me that a bird could
shatter a windscreen – though, of course, it could. The vision
was complete, instantaneous; it can't have taken longer than a
few seconds for the whole thing – both scenarios, the
devastating one and the 'better' one – to flash past my inner
sight. And it was clear, spontaneous, and extremely graphic: I
saw everything, and felt it: the blow, the shock, the fright.

Two minutes later, no more, this happened. A bird – or
something – hit the corner of the car, just by the windscreen on
the passenger side, with a huge, loud, sudden THWACK. I

immediately assumed it was a bird, and gasped out loud. It could have been an object rather than a bird – but I was probably driving too fast for any thrown object to connect, and I didn't notice anyone who could have thrown anything: there was no other car near me, and no-one, so far as I'm aware, standing by the roadside. On the other hand, there was no blood when I checked later, only the twisted, wizened rubber protective tubing between the roof and the windscreen. The noise, the impact of the blow was a stunning shock. My feelings, as I drove along, are indescribable. My first thought was: I brought that on, by imagining it so vividly. Then I thought, no, I simply *foresaw* it. I was stunned, both by the blow and the thought, and I remember telling myself to concentrate on my driving. After a while I assigned the word 'precognition' to it. I mentioned it briefly to Swamiji when I arrived, and told Klaus about it when I got home.

Then I forgot all about it until this morning. When Klaus, having washed the windscreen for me, remarked how strange, melted, the damaged tubing looked where whatever it was had struck it, I thought about it again, how strange the whole experience had been. And then I thought, it had been a statement, a message, about my cancer and my future. Something like this: 'The worst didn't happen. It wasn't a fatal accident/illness. Your life has not been shattered. And the "better", middle scenario didn't happen either. Nothing has been shattered. It was just a glancing blow – a shock, but no great, no lasting damage. No bloodshed, no devastation, no danger – just a glancing blow.'

Other thoughts occurred. That I had perhaps, by 'seeing' the incident before it happened, brought it about, made it happen. Or, by seeing it and then imagining a 'better' way for it to happen, deflected it. But no – it wasn't *me*, it wasn't my doing. What happened was what happened, it happened exactly as it happened. Both the vision and the blow were part of the happening, the experience.

I take it as a sign. Confirmation, that what happened to me was *not* the worst thing, not even the halfway thing, but only a glancing blow. *Only a glancing blow.* The shock was sudden, the damage severe, but *contained*: limited, confined to a small area. There were no repercussions. There will be no repercussions, and no recurrence.

The feeling was so sure, so strong, that for a while I considered calling this book *A Glancing Blow*. And it has remained, that powerful sense that my cancer was just that: a glancing blow.

Will my cancer really not ever recur? I don't know: how could I? Will I live as long as I want to – another thirty years? Perhaps, and perhaps not. Life gives no guarantees. Breast cancer is a funny thing: its micro-metastases, its 'seedlings', can lurk in the bloodstream and take hold as cancerous tumours anywhere in the body at any time; soon after the first illness, or many years later. But if that happens to me, and if I die sooner than I want to, neither event will negate my healing, as I have come to understand healing.

The impulse that fuelled my healing was surrender, acceptance: surrender to God and acceptance of cancer, acceptance of death and dying, acceptance of life's uncertainties. I am content with things as they are, with things as they are to be. Cancer has not been a battle for me. It has been and will continue to be a healing process, fed by the willingness to go through the experience and not evade it. I have tried to own it, tried not to waste precious energy in denial and self-deception. So far I think I have succeeded, more or less.

It's now two years since my lump was diagnosed as cancer. Towards the end of the first year, someone said to me, 'Well, I suppose you can scratch this year, just quietly forget all about it.' But I didn't, and I don't, want to forget about it. That first year of cancer, which at the beginning promised to be the most difficult year of my life, was in every important way enriching. The whole experience of cancer and healing has sent me forward into my life with more to offer than I had before.

A month after my mastectomy, I found myself telling a friend that if I were offered the chance to turn the clock back, I would refuse. I said: 'If someone had asked me, "how would you like to get breast cancer and learn all about life and death?" I would have said "no thanks". But it has happened, and I wouldn't change it.'

Hearing myself say this, I was surprised. But it was true, and it still is. I don't want to go back. I am content.

8   Using Our Breath to Help Us

**Breath is life and life is breath;
so long as there is breath in the body there is life.**

Kaushitaki Upanishad

All through my experience of cancer, the simple breathing exercises I have learned through yoga were an enormous help to me. They helped me to hold my balance and stay in touch with myself, and deal with my fears as I faced what was happening to me. I hope you too will find them helpful.

Our emotions affect our breathing. You may have observed that when you are happy and calm, your breathing is smooth and even. When you are anxious it becomes shallow and irregular. When you are frightened it is constricted, and you may feel tight in the chest.

What is not so well understood is that the opposite is also true. Our breathing pattern affects our nervous system, and through it, our emotions and state of mind. A disturbed breathing pattern can set in motion a vicious cycle in which anxiety mounts, fear turns to panic. Fortunately, this process also works the other way. By becoming aware of our breathing pattern, and by consciously, but not forcibly, changing it, we help to calm the sympathetic nervous system. Thus we can use our breath to help us let go of anxiety and stress, avert panic and restore calm and balance. We can use it to help us through the anxious days and nights around diagnosis, through post-operative pain and the discomforts of further treatment. We can use our breath to help us heal.

Most of us breathe automatically most of the time. We breathe shallowly and erratically, without being at all aware of our breath. Regular practice of simple exercises will help us to become more aware of the breath, and to establish a deeper, more rhythmic breathing pattern.

Physiologically, good breathing brings more oxygen into the blood for the body cells. When we breathe really well, utilizing the full capacity of our lungs, the respiratory system functions at its best. As a result, circulation, digestion and elimination also improve. The good functioning of all the body systems, and thus the quality of our life, depend on the quality of our breathing. When we feel physically better, our state of mind is transformed.

Mentally and emotionally, good breathing releases tension and calms the mind, nerves and emotions. It helps to overcome fatigue and replenish energy. It improves sleep, memory, concentration and all our mental processes.

Spiritually, breath brings energy into our being. It carries the life force throughout the body and connects all the levels of our being: physical, mental, and spiritual. Our breath is the vital link between body, mind and spirit, and between ourselves and all creation.

Breath awareness

During the first fortnight of November 1993, between my first visit to my doctor and my diagnosis, I would start violently out of sleep at 2 or 3am with the full weight of what was happening bearing down upon me. Going back to sleep wasn't possible, but if I lay there letting my emotions wash over me they quickly swamped me: I needed a little distance from them to be able to handle them.

So I would get out of bed, go to my work room, switch on the electric heater and sit down to practise breath awareness.

This natural, simple practice calms and steadies us, and helps us to centre ourselves. It is the foundation of many of the meditation practices in the Buddhist, Islamic and Christian traditions. It is the heart and soul of yoga.

Breath awareness allows us to experience yoga in its most basic yet most profound sense. As the emotions are calmed, and the restless movements of the mind brought to rest, we are led towards the peace and stillness that are in fact always within us, but obscured by the incessant activity of our mind and emotions. When we breathe with full awareness of our breath, we draw together all our scattered forces. We concentrate energy so that it can be channelled rather than dissipated, utilized rather than squandered.

Breath awareness helps us develop the inner strength, evenness of mind and detachment that we need to hold our own in crisis. It has been the foundation of my practice for many years, and I know now, better than ever, how completely it can be relied upon in times of stress.

The small hours, when you are most likely to need the help the practice can give, are in fact the best possible time for it. (I only wish I had the self-discipline to get up and practise at 3am now that urgent need no longer impels me to!) External noises are at a minimum, and distractions and interruptions are less likely. If you have a family they are probably still asleep, and as long as you can find a quiet corner and close a door behind you, you won't need to worry about disturbing them.

But of course you can practise breath awareness at any time. Just be sure of a block of time when you are not likely to be disturbed. Let your family know how important it is for you to take this time for yourself, and ask for their co-operation and support. Close the door and unplug the phone.

A word about sleep. I have never met anyone at the start of a cancer experience who did not find their sleeping pattern disrupted. If we are accustomed to sleeping through to morning, it is alarming to find ourselves waking regularly in the middle of the night. If we know we have to get up to go to work, or look after young children first thing in the morning, we will feel that we *must* go back to sleep, and we try.

But when we wake in dismay and dread in the middle of the night we are unlikely to be able to fall asleep again. If we lie there letting our anxieties mount, we may be overwhelmed by them. I felt it was better to get up at once. After an hour or so of being awake and using the wakeful time to practise and calm myself, I returned to bed and was then usually able to go back to sleep.

It's easier to confront our terrors from an upright position! We feel stronger and not so vulnerable as when we are lying down, and are better able to look at them and take charge of them.

Preliminaries

Before you begin, cry if you need to. Release any tears you may be holding back. Then get yourself into a comfortable seated position.

If you are familiar with any of the seated meditative postures and are comfortable sitting on the floor, you may do so, but this isn't necessary; you can sit in a chair. The important thing is not to slump, so choose one in which you can hold your spine upright: a straight-backed kitchen chair is better than an easy chair. Place your feet flat on the floor under your knees, hip-width apart. (If they dangle, rest them on a footstool or telephone directory.) Be sure you sit on the 'sitting bones' at the bottom of the pelvis, not on the base of your spine. Allow your spine and neck to lengthen up freely, and rest your hands comfortably in your lap. See figure 1.

Figure 1

If you want to sit cross-legged on the floor, sit on a firm cushion or telephone directory. This elevation will help avoid strain on the lower back and knees. Again, sit on your sitting bones, not on the base of your spine.

If you want to kneel, a tightly-rolled blanket between your thighs will elevate your hips, help keep your spine upright, and avoid restricting circulation in your legs.

Whichever position you choose, your body should be steady and comfortable, your spine upright and lengthened, not sagging. Take a few minutes to establish this. You are beginning to bring your body to stillness and steadiness. When the body is steady, the breath can grow steady, and then the activities of the mind begin to slow down.

Observe yourself gently and without judging for the following:

> spine upright
> shoulders soft, not hunched
> chest open
> mouth soft
> tongue resting gently in the mouth
> jaw heavy
> cheeks soft
> eyelids gently closed
> eyes soft
> forehead smooth
> hands soft in the lap

And now you're ready to begin.

Breath awareness

➤ Bring your attention to the space between the tip of the nose and the upper lip. Focus gently on the sensations as your breath flows over this space.

➤ Become aware of the breath flowing in and out of your nostrils. Don't change it, just be aware of it as it is.

➤ Be aware of the *temperature* of the breath. Notice that the inbreath is cool against the nostrils, the outbreath warmer.

➤ Be aware of the *depth* of the breath. It may be deep or shallow, or alternate between the two. Don't change it and don't judge it. Let it be as it is, and observe it.

➤ Be aware of the *rhythm* of the breath. Is it even or erratic; is it flowing freely or it is somewhat restricted?

➤ Be aware of the *quality* of the breath. Is it quiet or noisy, smooth or ragged?

➤ Don't change the breath and don't judge it. Just observe it quietly, and accept whatever you find.

When you have been having strong feelings, and perhaps crying, the breath may be restricted and its rhythm unsteady. Your chest may feel tight, especially if you have been holding on to the feelings. Don't try to change the breath, just keep your attention focused on it. Observe it as it is. Gradually it will begin to grow smoother, steadier.

➤ Now become more aware of the outbreath. Let it flow out fully and completely, let it take as long as it needs. As you do this, have a sense of letting go, of releasing, of surrendering.

➤ Let the outbreath go on for as long as it wants to: don't anticipate the end of it.

➤ When exhalation is full and complete, inhalation deepens naturally. So now be aware of the breath flowing in, a little deeper, smoother and calmer.

➤ Don't 'try', don't strain or pull at the breath. Don't make an effort, just allow the breath to deepen gradually.

➤ As you allow the breath to deepen, become aware of your abdomen, and let it be soft, don't hold it tense. Notice its movements as your breath deepens, how it moves forward gently with the inbreath, and comes back to rest with the outbreath. Don't do anything to influence these movements, just let them happen, and be aware of them.

➤ With each exhalation, empty yourself and let go of tension and anxiety.

➤ Then welcome in a new breath of life.

➤ Each exhalation is cleansing your being of waste, used stale air, and toxins, releasing tension, stress and anxiety. Each inhalation is nourishing your being, filling it with energy and life force.

➤ When you are ready to end the practice, move and stretch the body gently, first your fingers and toes, then your arms and legs, before standing up.

As you get into this practice and begin to release tension, your feelings will come up. This is the purpose of the practice, so don't treat it as an unwelcome interruption. At first, they will probably come up pretty quickly. The fears that have been pressing on you, the sorrow or anger or bitterness you may have been trying to avoid feeling, will put themselves before you. Don't ignore them, don't push them away. Let them be there.

This isn't a time for analysing feelings, just for letting them surface into consciousness and gently observing them. The clarity, detachment and insight gained through simply sitting still and looking is all that is needed to release the feelings and the energy that has been blocked in them.

Imagine that the emotions are passing across a screen in front of you. Just watch them as you continue to follow the flow of your breath. If you find yourself getting involved with them and trying to analyse them or 'work things out', remind yourself gently to just let them be there.

You need to acknowledge your emotions, and own them, in order to release them, and this is your opportunity to begin doing that. Whatever you feel, try not to judge it: it's what you feel and it's all right.

Try not to label your feelings as 'good' or 'bad'. Just begin to know what they are, and to accept them. Welcome them in and begin to learn to distinguish between them.

If you start to cry, don't try to stop the tears, thinking you're supposed to be getting on with the practice, because crying is what you need to do now. As it is not really possible to cry and practise breath awareness at the same time, you'll have to let go of breath awareness for a bit, and just cry!

Cry without holding back, so that the tears can do their job of releasing your feelings. You may find that you sigh a great deal, you may want to bury your face in your hands, or lean forward, or lie down on your stomach. Do whatever feels natural. But don't get hooked into the feelings, don't start thinking and analysing. Just let the tears cleanse away a little of that pent-up feeling that has been building inside, let them wash it out of you. Let it go, release it.

Don't be afraid of the tears. If you are inclined to be brave and strong and to hold your tears back, either to spare others having to cope with your feelings or to avoid them yourself, crying may feel like an uncontrollable opening of the floodgates. You might be afraid that once you start you'll never be able to stop. But you will.

Do keep an eye on yourself to make sure you aren't whipping yourself up into a frenzy of emotion, that you aren't making it more intense than it is. Be ready to stop crying when the tears have done their work. Don't anticipate this moment, but don't over-shoot it either.

You may find that it doesn't take very long for the crying to stop. As soon as you are calmer, re-establish your upright sitting posture and return to observing your breath. Now that you have released some of the pressure and tension inside you, you may find that your breath is steadier than it was before. It may be deeper. However it is, just be aware of it as it is now.

This process may or may not repeat itself. You may need to cry again, or you may not. Just stay with the process, whatever happens, finishing with breath awareness. By now you may feel calm enough to go back to bed, and you may find that you now fall into a deeper, quieter sleep.

You can practise breath awareness at any time, wherever you are and whenever you remember – waiting for the bus, on the bus, in the supermarket queue. It will be helpful while travelling to or waiting for consultations, tests and treatment, occasions on which anxiety tends to mount.

After some time spent practising breath awareness you will find yourself developing a measure of steadiness and clarity that will help you to keep your balance on the cancer roller-coaster ride. Over a longer period you will find these attributes increasing, and your practice bearing fruits you did not anticipate. What began as a form of first aid for sleepless nights will have become an integral part of your life, nourishing and sustaining and transforming it.

More breathing exercises

Simple breathing exercises can greatly improve our general health. Combined with stretching movements they restore elasticity and strength to our diaphragm and intercostal muscles and improve the depth and quality of our breathing. When we breathe more fully and slowly, our intake of oxygen is increased, our energy levels are raised, and the functioning of all our body systems is improved. Breathing exercises concentrate energy and relieve tension, anxiety and stress.

The following sequences all involve simple stretching movements, co-ordinated with the breath. Along with breath awareness, co-ordination of movement and breath is the keynote of yoga practice.

When we co-ordinate breath and movement in a flowing, rhythmic way, we bring balance and harmony into our whole being.

When you practise, be aware of the natural rhythm of your own breath. Allow the breath to lead the movement and do not hold the breath. Breathe in and out through the nostrils unless otherwise instructed, or if a cold or other respiratory problem makes that impossible. The nostrils warm and purify the air before we take it into the lungs.

You can do these exercises whenever you have a few minutes – while you're waiting for the kettle to boil, for example.

The full breath 1

➤ Stand tall, but easy and relaxed, feet hip-width apart and parallel, tailbone tucked under, shoulders not hunched up, mouth and eyes soft, and a soft feeling at the backs of the knees. See figure 2.

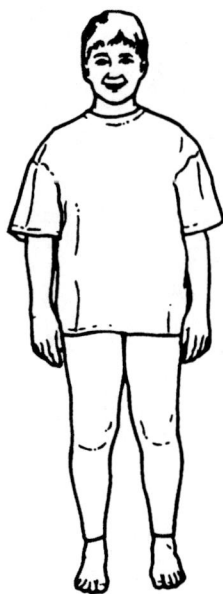

➤ Exhale gently.

Figure 2

➤ Inhale as you raise your arms to the front, keeping them parallel, till your fingertips point toward the ceiling. Avoid hollowing your lower back. See figure 3.

➤ Exhale as you lower your arms.

➤ Do this three to five times, co-ordinating the movement with the breath.

➤ Work gently, with awareness of the breath and movement. Do not force the breath. Just allow it to flow, and let the movement follow it. There should be no strain.

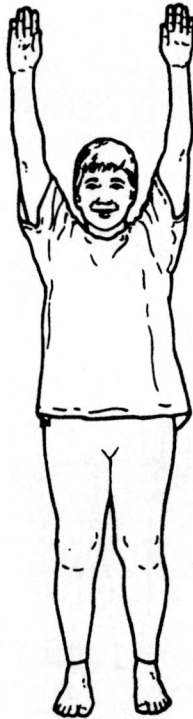

Figure 3

The full breath 2

➤ Stand tall, but easy and relaxed, your feet hip width apart and parallel, tailbone tucked under, shoulders down, mouth and eyes soft, and a soft feeling at the backs of the knees. Exhale gently.

➤ Turn your arms out, all the way from your shoulders, and feel this movement opening your chest.

➤ Inhale as you raise your arms to the sides, keeping them straight if possible. Press your palms together. See figure 4.

➤ Then turn your arms – from the shoulders – and bring the backs of your hands together.

➤ Exhale as you lower your arms to your sides.

➤ Do this three to five times, co-ordinating movement and breath.

Figure 4

The sunburst breath

Stress and anxiety restrict our breathing, and make it shallow and erratic. When we notice this, our impulse may be to take a deep breath *in*. But it is more helpful to breathe fully *out*, to empty the lungs with a strong, vigorous exhalation. A deeper, fuller inbreath will follow naturally.

The sunburst breath combines a forceful exhalation with a lovely up-and-backward stretch.

> Stand tall, but easy and relaxed, as before. Tuck your tailbone under and squeeze your buttocks to support your lower back during the exercise.

> Exhale gently.

> Inhale as you raise your arms in front, keeping them parallel. Fingers point toward the ceiling, palms face forward. Stretch up, without hollowing your lower back. See figure 5.

> Exhale through the mouth with a sigh, as you lift your chest and stretch backward, opening your arms to a 'V' shape. See figure 6.

> Inhaling, come upright and stretch up.

> Exhaling normally, lower your arms to the front.

> Keep your buttocks firm throughout, to support your lower back.

> Don't throw your head back: keep your ears between your arms as you stretch up and back so that you don't compress your neck.

> This is one round. Do three to five rounds in all.

Figure 5

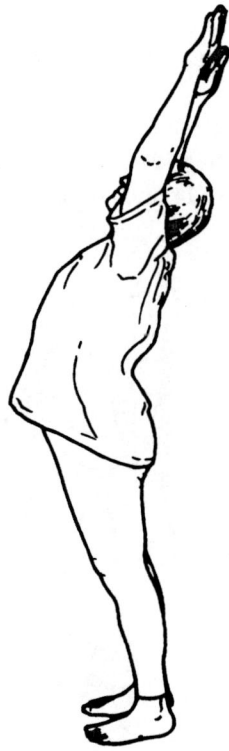

Figure 6

Curling and stretching

This is an enjoyable, relaxed and relaxing sequence of movements, marvellous for releasing tension in the whole body, and especially in the spine, neck and shoulders, and the hands and arms.

If you find it difficult at first to co-ordinate the movements with the breath as instructed, just breathe naturally, but don't hold your breath. Gradually you will find a rhythm is established as the movements begin to fit in with your breathing.

➤ Stand as before, tall, but easy and relaxed. Let your arms hang loose.

➤ Tuck in your chin and bend your knees a little. Exhale as you curl down towards the floor. Let your arms dangle, and keep your chin tucked in. See figure 7.

➤ Curl down as far as you can comfortably, letting your hands, arms, shoulders and neck go soft. You don't have to go all the way to the floor. Feel that your trunk and arms and head are heavy and floppy – like a rag doll's. See figures 8 and 9.

➤ Inhaling, begin to curl up, using your back muscles to lift your trunk. Feel them working, and feel the stretch across your back. Let your arms and hands dangle as they follow your body up.

Figure 7

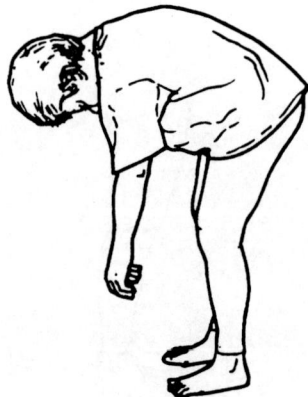

Figure 8

➤ Bend your elbows, keeping them close to your body. Continue inhaling as you stretch your arms up above your head, palms facing each other. See figure 10.

➤ Feel you are stretching from the soles of your feet to your fingertips, like a rubber band being pulled out at both ends. See figure 11.

➤ Exhaling, turn your arms so your elbows face forward. Curl your hands loosely and bend your elbows, keeping them close to your body. Tuck in your chin and curl down once more.

➤ Repeat these movements a few more times, curling down on the outbreath, stretching up on the inbreath (if you find this difficult at first, just breathe naturally). Feel your body growing softer and more relaxed each time you curl down, and more elastic each time you stretch up.

Figure 9   *Figure 10*   *Figure 11*

The nine pacifying breaths

This sequence is performed with three arm movements, all co-ordinated with full, rhythmic breathing. It calms the nervous system, and will leave you feeling poised and balanced, centred and ready to take control. It is a useful exercise to practise at any time, but especially when faced with any situation that makes you feel anxious. It helps afterwards, too, to restore balance and calm. It can also help relieve insomnia if practised before going to sleep.

➤ Stand tall, but easy and relaxed.

➤ Centre yourself by observing your breath for a few moments. Close your eyes if you wish. Let everything else recede from your mind so that you can absorb yourself completely in the movements.

➤ Exhale gently, and take your arms a little out to the sides.

➤ Inhale as you cross your arms in front of you, and raise them till they are straight (as if you're taking off a tight pullover). See figure 12.

Figure 12

➤ Turn your arms so your palms face out. Breathe out and lower your arms. Without breaking the rhythm, cross them again in front of your chest.

➤ Do this three more times, in rhythm with the breath.

➤ Now turn your arms out from your shoulders so that your palms face out. Inhale and raise your arms up and over your head, bringing your palms together. See figure 13.

➤ Turn your arms out from the shoulders and bring the backs of your hands together. Exhale and lower your arms to your sides.

➤ Do this two more times, synchronizing movement and breath.

➤ Then turn your arms so that your palms face forward. Inhale and raise your arms, keeping them parallel, palms up, until your fingertips point towards the ceiling, palms facing backward. See figure 14.

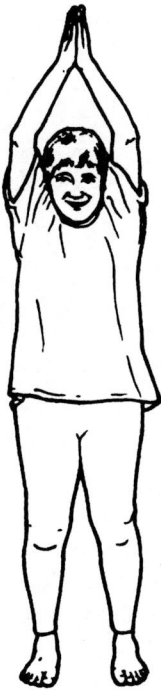

Figure 13   Figure 14

➤ Turn your arms so your palms face forward. Breathing out, lower your arms to the front.

➤ Do this once more.

➤ Now stand still for a few moments, and observe your breath. You will probably find that you are breathing more slowly, and more deeply, than you were before.

➤ When you feel ready to do so, open your eyes.

An audio cassette tape is available to accompany this chapter and the next. Please write to Julie Friedeberger, c/o Element Books Ltd, Longmead, Shaftesbury, Dorset SP7 8PL, enclosing a cheque or postal order for £7.50 (£8.50 outside the U.K.).

And Indra continued:
'I am Prana, the life breath,
and the consciousness in all beings.
Glorify me, for I am life and I am immortality.
Life is breath and breath is life.
So long as there is breath in the body, there is life.
From Prana comes the nectar of life,
and from consciousness comes clear understanding.
He who glorifies me as the life breath,
in this life enjoys fullness
and in the next immortality, eternity.

One can live without speech, for there are the dumb.
One can live without sight, for there are the blind.
One can live without hearing, for there are the deaf.
One can live without thought, for there are the simple.
One can live without limbs, for there are the crippled.
But one cannot live without breath.

It is Prana alone, as the conscious Self,
that breathes life into this body.
So to Prana we should sing all hymns of praise.
Prana is the esssence of the life breath.
And what is the life breath?
It is pure consciousness.
And what is pure consciousness?
It is the life breath.'

                              Kaushitaki Upanishad

9   Learning to Let Go: Deep Relaxation

> As soon as a person understands what has been said
> to him for his good, he has no further need to hear
> or discuss, but to set himself in earnest to practise
> what he has learnt with silence and attention.

I recalled this passage from the letters of St John of the Cross in June
when, a couple of months after I had returned to teaching, Peter
Harrison, a teaching colleague told me: 'Your immune system will be
happy and will function efficiently if you are at peace within yourself. If
you aren't, it won't. So you must make it your absolute priority to bring
yourself to stillness as often as possible.'

Many who have written about illness and recovery take the view
that deep relaxation is by far the most important single element in
healing, and that the regular practice of relaxation is the most valuable
thing we can do for ourselves. I had been practising it consistently, but
since my return to teaching I had become lax. It wasn't that I 'didn't
have time'. The time was there, but as I had foreseen, my attention and
energy were now directed outward: it wasn't easy for me to shift gears
and look within. My period of retreat, quiet, rest, contemplation was
over. I was busy again, and it was more difficult to stop moving and
come to rest. I was engaged with life and with the world outside myself;
I was thinking more and more about teaching, and beginning, just a
little, to lose touch with my own needs. The deepest and most urgent
of these was time for myself, time for stillness, but I was allowing myself
less and less of it.

So I needed Peter's reminder, and heeded it. I reinstated daily
relaxation as my absolute priority and have made it so ever since.

Most mornings, first thing, I spend at least half an hour flat on my
back on the floor. Morning is a good time. The mind is at its quietest;
it hasn't been filled with words and thoughts. If I do it first, nothing
can take priority over it. It gets the day off to a good start, and leaves

the whole day ahead, in which it is often possible to find time to do it again. The more, the better. Relaxation is vital – for everyone, in any state of health, but especially for anyone who is coping with serious illness.

Peter Harrison says:

Deep down within each one of us, there is a silent, wise intelligence responsible for the entire health of the whole being, the health of the body, the health of the emotions, the health of the mind. In order to co-operate with this silent, wise intelligence, we need to let go of all else that would absorb our attention and would use up our precious energy... This silent, wise intelligence, responsible for the entire health of the whole body, works at its most efficient in those moments of deep and total relaxation. In this deep relaxation we are not aware of our problems of the day, we are not aware of any tensions, we know of no pain, no sorrow, no frustrations, and there are no desires to be fulfilled. This is the blessing, the importance, of deep and total relaxation. [15]

Relaxation isn't something we 'do'. It is a complete letting go, a surrender of one's body and of all the activity of one's mind, a giving up. It's the cessation of doing, the exact opposite of doing. Relaxation helps to overcome tension and discomfort in the body, anxieties and disturbances in the mind.

Relaxation is coming to rest in the stillness within. In bringing ourselves into this stillness, in contacting that 'silent, wise intelligence' within, we encourage our inner healing forces to work for us, and prepare the most fertile ground for them to work in. In deep relaxation, healing takes place.

Few people know what it is really to relax. The very word 'relax', when given as an instruction – or even as a friendly suggestion – is more than likely to have the opposite effect. If we've had it drummed into us by friends, partners or doctors that we 'ought to relax more', and we've found it impossible or think we're too busy even to try, being told to 'relax' can make us even more tense (and probably irritable as well).

For those who find it difficult to relax, it is comforting to know that relaxation is a skill that can be learned like any other. And it is worth learning. Relaxation relieves stress-related conditions and improves sleep. In relaxation the heart rate and blood pressure drop, the breathing slows down, and the muscles let go of tension. In time, the activities of the mind also slow down; tension and anxiety begin to dissolve. With body and mind at rest, our burdens lifted, we move toward stillness, peace and harmony.

This isn't an illusion. These states of being aren't something outside us that we have to go in search of, they are there within us, waiting for us to touch them. Physical, emotional and mental disturbances, even most of our daily activities with all their hustle and bustle and pressure, obscure the stillness within us. Relaxation dissolves all these impediments and leads us to it.

Nor are the spells of peace and stillness we experience in relaxation merely enjoyable fleeting interludes between our more 'normal' periods of turmoil and stress. The effects of relaxation are cumulative and lasting, and with regular practice we will observe changes in ourselves, perhaps even a transformation of our habitual ways of being. Each time we go into a deeply relaxed state we learn something about letting go, and this learning stays with us; just as a miner, going down into the mine, brings more gold back to the surface each time.

In fact, we learn detachment, which we need in order to gain any clear understanding of our emotions. Regular practice of relaxation, by repeatedly getting us off the treadmill of emotion, preoccupation and activity, can help us develop detachment.

In relaxation we aren't 'doing' anything. Our lives are full of doing, and all our doing, necessary though it is, inevitably creates tensions and difficulties. Relaxation is un-doing, letting the world go about its business, trusting that it can manage for a while without our input. In relaxation we discover that it is not only all right but a rare pleasure, just to *be*. Each time you practise relaxation, each time you let go of tension and anxiety for a while, your being comes to rest in the stillness and space you create for yourself, and you experience the joy of 'just being'.

Mastery of relaxation techniques enables us to deal more effectively and more creatively with the responsibilities, demands and duties of life, and helps us to overcome hindrances to peace of mind. In letting go of tensions in body and mind we surrender ourselves. Gradually and subtly our attitude and approach to life begin to change. Deeper levels of consciousness are reached, and we are led towards inner transformation.

The most essential condition for relaxation is the assurance that you won't be disturbed. Choose a time of day when you know you will be left to yourself, and if necessary enlist your family's co-operation and support: explain that it's important you take this time for yourself. Close the door and disconnect the telephone.

Warmth is also necessary. The room temperature should be about 70 degrees F (21 degrees C). If this isn't feasible, your clothing must be warm enough to allow for the drop in body temperature which occurs when you are lying still. Even in summer you will usually need socks, and perhaps a pullover.

The room should also be quiet, if possible, although you are less in control of that element. If you have to put up with noise outside or inside the house, it can help to remember that noise is part of life and that we can't always expect our environment to be exactly as we'd like it. Be aware of the noises, and don't try to shut them out, but do not get involved with them. Just let them go on, and keep returning your awareness to what you are doing.

The surface for relaxation should be firm and even to provide good support for the spine. A carpeted floor is ideal, otherwise use a thick mat or folded blanket on a bare floor. The ground outdoors is too uneven, and all but the very firmest beds are too soft, to be suitable.

First you need to know how to lie down. Relaxing doesn't mean flopping! You need to place yourself on the floor carefully, without pulling your spine out of line.

The posture used for relaxation is called Shavasana. In English it is known as the corpse pose, and it is considered the most important yoga posture of all.

➤ Sit with your legs straight in front of you, your spine upright.

➤ Bend your knees, hug them to you, and stretch your spine up.

➤ Put your hands on the floor a little behind your hips, fingers forward.

➤ Look down: line up your nose between your big toes.

➤ Tuck in your chin, and slowly curl your spine down onto the floor.

➤ Keep your nose lined up between your big toes and keep your chin tucked in: avoid letting your head drop back.

➤ Rest for awhile with your knees bent, heels close to the buttocks (this releases tension in the lower back).

➤ Slowly straighten your legs one at a time, sliding your heels along the floor. Let your feet fall out to the sides: they should be a foot or so apart.

➤ Turn your arms out and bring the backs of your hands onto the floor, palms facing up.

➤ Upper arms should be a little away from the ribcage, shoulders sinking gently into the floor. If this doesn't 'feel right', rest your hands gently on your abdomen.

➤ Be sure you feel balanced and aligned, that the weight is evenly distributed on both sides of the spine and your head is centred, not tilting to one side.

Note: If you feel pain or discomfort in your lower back after you straighten your legs, bend your knees again. A little extra time with knees bent often brings about the necessary release, and then you can try again. Alternatively a rolled-up towel placed just under the backs of the knees may give sufficient relief. If you find your chin poking up you need something under your head – a firm cushion or a paperback book or two – to avoid your neck getting squashed and tense.

This may sound like a lot of trouble to go to to lie down, but it only takes a few minutes, and by doing it carefully and attentively you have already created suitable conditions for relaxation by ensuring that your spine is aligned and lengthened and that you are balanced physically, which will encourage emotional and mental balance as well as release of tensions.

Here are three relaxation techniques that I have found particularly effective in my own practice and teaching. They furnish us with different methods of releasing tension and letting go of anxiety, and can be used individually or together, depending on the length of time you have available. They can also be used to help you get to sleep at night.

Releasing tension with the outbreath

The first technique is a sequence of simple breathing exercises, using four different types of exhalation to release tension. It can be done as a short practice on its own, or as preparation for either of the other two (or any others you may know that work for you).

Most of us, if we think about breathing at all, would say that the important bit is breathing in. Of course it is important – but breathing out is even more so. Full, complete exhalation empties our lungs of the maximum amount of stale, impurity-laden air. We never empty them completely: there is always some residual air. But exhaling fully expels more of it, and brings about a better exchange of gases so that it isn't always the same old stale air left behind to accumulate and cause disease. When exhalation is full and deep and wholly efficient, inhalation deepens naturally and effortlessly.

This sequence of four cleansing breaths utilizes increasingly strong exhalations to bring about deeper breathing and to release tension. It is also an opportunity to acknowledge and release pent-up feelings such as anger and resentment, and to express them harmlessly.

> *Let off steam if you must, but don't make anyone the target.*
> Swami Sivananda Radha

Anger, rage, hostility, resentment and bitterness are simply energy, manifesting as 'negative' emotions. We know from the laws of physics that energy cannot be created or destroyed, it can only be transformed. The energy trapped in negative feelings can be transformed by acknowledging and releasing them, but if we bury them through fear of feeling or expressing them they will fester and grow and become destructive. At the other extreme, if we express them thoughtlessly, if we direct them impulsively at our friends and loved ones, we will hurt them, and ourselves as well.

Between these two extremes there is a middle way, a gentler way: we can learn to acknowledge and look at our feelings, and release the energy held in them without hurting anyone.

When we can acknowledge and release our fear, our anger and frustration without making anyone a target for them, without injuring others or ourselves, without setting destructive vibrations in motion, the energy trapped in them can be transformed into healing energy.

This breathing sequence helps us to do that (and if all this sounds strange, don't worry; just notice how much better you feel after doing it!) It also brings about the deeper, more rhythmic breathing which improves the functioning of all your body systems and therefore your general health, and it brings body and mind to a state conducive to relaxation. It can be used at any time to release tension and anxiety quickly.

> **Caution: If you have high blood pressure, epilepsy or heart problems, please go gently with these exercises. The exhalations are quite strong, especially the last two.**

Bring yourself into Shavasana carefully and make sure that you feel comfortable, balanced and aligned. If you need to move and adjust yourself or your clothing to be sure of being comfortable, take a few moments to do that.

We begin with awareness of the body and of the breath.

➤ Become aware of the body. Become aware of the contact between the body and the floor.

➤ Be aware of the weight of the body, supported by the floor.

➤ Feel the firm floor beneath you, supporting you.

➤ Trust the floor to take the weight of your body. Know that you are supported, secure and safe.

➤ Become aware of the breath as it flows in and out of the nostrils. Don't change the breath: just be aware of it.

➤ Be aware of the temperature of the breath: the coolness of the inbreath, the warmth of the outbreath.

➤ Be aware of the rhythm of the breath. Is it smooth and even, or unsteady and jerky? Don't change it or judge it, just observe it, and accept what you find.

➤ Be aware of the depth of the breath. Don't change it, just observe it.

➤ Be aware of the gentle movements of the abdomen – rising as the breath comes in, gently subsiding as the breath goes out.

➤ Gradually increase the depth of the breath.

➤ With each outbreath, let go of tension and discomfort.

➤ With each inbreath, feel yourself being filled with life force, energy and vitality.

1 Inhale deeply, without 'trying' and without strain.

➤ *Sigh* the breath out, opening your mouth wide.

➤ Then allow the breath to flow in, slowly and deeply, with no strain.

➤ Repeat this two more times. With each sigh, allow your body to sink into the floor. Let go of tension and discomfort.

➤ (Gently pull in on your lower abdominal muscles towards the end of each outbreath. This pushes your diaphragm up and helps to expel maximum stale air.)

2 Inhale fully and deeply.

➤ *Blow* the breath out through a small hole in the lips, as if you were whistling.

➤ Do this three times, pulling in on the lower abdominal muscles towards the end of each exhalation and consciously expelling anxieties and worries.

3 Inhale deeply and this time hold the breath in for about three seconds.

➤ Smile widely and show your teeth: you should feel all your facial muscles working.

➤ *Hiss* the breath out through your lightly clenched teeth, loudly and forcefully.

➤ Carry on making this hissing sound until it stops by itself. This will take longer than you think, so don't anticipate, just keep hissing.

➤ Hiss strongly, vigorously. The sound will be like steam escaping from a pressure cooker. Do it with a clear sense that you are expelling the pressures within you. Be aware of any anger, bitterness or resentment you may be holding onto. Use this hissing breath to express them harmlessly: release them.

➤ Do this three times. Toward the end of each exhalation, gently pull in on the lower abdominal muscles.

4 Inhale deeply and hold, if possible for five seconds. If that's too long for you, hold for just three seconds.

➤ Then expel the breath forcefully through the open mouth, making the audible sound 'Hah!' This strong exhalation will expel large amounts of stale air, laden with impurities and toxins. Toward the end of the exhalation, gently pull in on the lower abdominal muscles.

➤ As you do this cleansing breath, feel that you are discarding any worn-out attitudes you may be aware of, any old, unhelpful behaviour patterns that are no longer appropriate for you.

➤ Feel you are cleansing your being of everything that is stale. Empty your lungs and your being of all that you no longer need, all that is no longer helpful in your life. Make room for a new breath of life, new energy, to flow into your being.

➤ Do this three times.

After completing this sequence of breaths, just lie quietly for a few minutes, observing your breath. Once again, be aware of the rhythm of the breath, its depth and quality. Be aware of any changes that have taken place in your breathing. Develop awareness of your body, and be aware of how you are feeling now.

If you are using this sequence on its own as a quick method for releasing tension, have a stretch, and then hug your knees and rock gently from side to side before you get up.

You may also use it as a preliminary to either or both of the relaxation practices that follow.

A simple relaxation technique: tensing and releasing muscles

Sometimes we may lie down for relaxation only to find that our muscles are so tense that we just lie there holding on to the tension and feeling more and more uncomfortable. This happens because very tense muscles can't let go of their tension just like that: first they need to be gently stretched. If you are tense, you will find it easier to relax if you first do some simple stretching movements.

A quick and effective way of doing this is to work through the major muscle groups, deliberately and systematically creating more tension in them in order to release it.

Again we begin in Shavasana, so please refer to the instructions for lying down. Be in a position of alignment and balance, leaving your knees bent for a little while to release any tension in the lower back.

After each of the following actions, take a few moments to register the new sensations in that part of your body.

Hands

➤ Inhale deeply as you stretch your right hand, palm facing up. Spread your fingers wide and feel the stretch across the palm.

➤ Exhale completely – sigh, if you like – and release the stretch, letting the hand go limp and soft. Do this three times.

➤ Then stretch and release the left hand three times.

➤ Then both hands together three times.

Arms and shoulders

➤ Inhale as you pull your right shoulder down away from your ear. Feel the stretch across the top of the shoulder and through the arm.

➤ Exhale and release, letting your shoulder sink into the floor. Do this three times.

➤ Then stretch and release the left shoulder three times, and then both shoulders together, three times.

➤ Inhale and squeeze your shoulder blades together.

➤ Exhale and release. Do this three times.

Spine

➤ Inhale and arch your lower back very gently.

➤ Exhale and let the lower back sink into the floor.

➤ Do this three times.

Legs

➤ Inhale as you stretch your right heel forward, as if pushing against a wall. Feel the stretch through the Achilles tendon, calf and thigh.

➤ Exhale and release the stretch, letting the foot fall out to the side.

➤ Do this three times.

➤ Then stretch and release the left leg three times, and then both legs together, three times.

Pelvic area

➤ Inhale as you squeeze your buttocks together, and pull up on the pelvic floor and anus.

➤ Exhale and release, letting your buttocks sink back into the floor. Do this three times.

Face

➤ Inhale deeply. Retain the breath for a few seconds as you tense your facial muscles. Make a 'funny face': purse your mouth, wrinkle your nose, screw up your eyes, as if you wanted to make them all disappear into the centre of your face.

➤ Exhale and release. Do this three times.

Whole body and face together

➤ Inhale deeply. Stretch your arms and hands and legs together. At the same time squeeze your buttocks. At the end of the inbreath tense your facial muscles. Now every muscle in your body is under tension. Hold the tension, and the breath, for a few seconds.

➤ Then exhale and release all the tension, letting your whole body sink into the floor.

➤ Do this three times.

➤ Then let go completely. Be aware of your whole body, heavy and supported by the floor, everything calm and still, quiet and at rest.

➤ Be aware of your breath, flowing in and out of your nostrils. Don't try to control or change it, just allow it to flow naturally and peacefully in and out, like the ebbing and flowing of the tide.

➤ Surrender each outbreath. Surrender your body to the support of the floor.

➤ Remain still for a few minutes, longer if you wish, observing the flow of your breath.

➤ Develop awareness of your body and of how you are feeling now. Experience and enjoy the new sensations brought about by releasing and letting go.

Coming back from relaxation

➤ When you are ready to get up, please don't hurry. Take time to make the transition between stillness and action.

➤ One by one, become aware of your senses: touch, taste, smell, hearing, and sight.

➤ Become aware of the contact between your body and the floor.

➤ Swallow gently: become aware of taste in the mouth.

➤ Begin to breathe more deeply: be aware of the sense of smell.

➤ Become aware of the sounds all around you.

➤ Become aware of the darkness behind your closed eyelids, and then of the light filtering through them.

➤ Now become aware of your surroundings: the space around the body, the whole of the room.

➤ Then begin to move your body, first gently curling and stretching your fingers and toes. Gently stretch your hands and gently stretch your heels away from you.

➤ Bring the sides of your feet together and your arms by your body, palms on the floor.

➤ Exhale and gently pull your shoulders down away from your ears.

➤ Inhale deeply as you stretch your arms up and back, bringing your hands to the floor behind your head. Sigh the breath out through your open mouth as you bring your arms down alongside you.

➤ Do this two more times.

➤ Bring your knees up onto your abdomen and give yourself a hug. Gently rock from side to side a few times.

➤ Roll over onto one side, and when you feel ready, ease yourself gently into a sitting position. Avoid any jerky or sudden movements that would disturb your sense of calm and your breath rhythm.

➤ Sit quietly for a few moments, observing your breath.

➤ Rub your palms briskly together and when they are warm, cup them very gently over your closed eyes. Let the warmth and energy from your palms flow through your eyelids into your eyes, soothing and healing, energizing and revitalizing. Open your eyes into your hands and gaze softly into the darkness. Then gently take your hands away.

Now that you have completed your relaxation, don't undo the good you've done by immediately jumping up and rushing around. Take your time, move slowly, look about you. Notice all you see, hear, taste, feel, and smell. Keep the good feeling as you go through your day.

Calming the nervous system

This simple, effective technique touches on sixteen major nerve zones. It is based on an ancient practice which has been handed down over the centuries. In focusing our awareness on certain key areas of the body, it releases tension and helps to calm the entire nervous system. Practised regularly it will help to detach your mind from worry and anxiety, relieve mental and emotional stress and bring about total rest and a sense of peace and well-being.

It is given as a separate practice, and can be done on its own, but if you feel very tense before you begin it you'll find it helpful to do one of the previous exercises first – the sequence of four cleansing breaths, or the tensing and releasing sequence, or both. You could also do some of the simple stretching and breathing exercises in Chapter 8.

The technique is a simple one in which you'll bring your awareness to each part of the body as it is named. You'll do this with an inbreath. Then, as you breathe out, you'll breathe away tension, you'll let go. You don't have to think about it, or 'concentrate'. Just allow your awareness to travel lightly from each part of the body to the next.

➤ Begin by lying down comfortably on the floor in Shavasana, following the instructions given on page 137.

➤ Feel you are lying with your weight evenly distributed on both sides of your spine. Your feet should be a comfortable distance apart, your arms a little away from your body, your shoulders resting on the floor, your palms facing the ceiling.

➤ Allow time to make any necessary adjustments to your body and your clothing. Do anything you need to do to allow you to lie still during the practice. Take your time. Give the body time to settle and grow steady.

➤ If your lower back is painful with your legs straight, bend your knees and rest your feet on the floor, hip-distance apart, fairly close to your buttocks, or place a rolled-up towel under the backs of your knees.

➤ Become aware of the body. Be aware of the contact between the body and the floor. Be aware of the weight of your body, supported by the floor. Allow the floor to support your body. Observe your body as it begins to grow steady and still.

➤ Sigh the breath out a few times, allowing the body to sink into the floor with each sigh.

➤ Then allow the breath to flow naturally and easily. Be aware of the breath as it flows. Don't change the breath, just be aware of it.

➤ Be aware of the temperature of the breath.

➤ Become aware of the depth of the breath, and the rhythm of the breath.

➤ With each outbreath, allow the body to melt into the floor.

Breathe in as you bring your awareness to your *feet*.
As you breathe out, let go.

Breathe in as you bring your awareness to your *shins*.
As you breathe out, let go.

Breathe in as you bring your awareness to your *kneecaps*.
As you breathe out, let go.

Breathe in as you bring your awareness to your *thighs*.
As you breathe out let go.

Breathe in as you bring your awareness to your *abdomen*.
As you breathe out, let go.

Breathe in as you bring your awareness to your *solar plexus*.
As you breathe out, let go.

Breathe in as you bring your awareness to your *upper chest*.
As you breathe out, let go.

Breathe in as you bring your awareness to your *spine*.
As you breathe out, let go.

Breathe in as you bring your awareness to your *hands*.
As you breathe out, let go.

Breathe in as you bring your awareness to your *forearms*.
As you breathe out, let go.

Breathe in as you bring your awareness to your *upper arms*.
As you breathe out, let go.

Breathe in as you bring your awareness to your *throat*.
As you breathe out, let go.

Breathe in as you bring your awareness to *the back of your head*.
As you breathe out, let go.

Breathe in as you bring your awareness to your *jaw*.
As you breathe out, let go.

Breathe in as you bring your awareness to your *eyes*.
As you breathe out, let go.

Breathe in as you bring your awareness to your *scalp*.
As you breathe out, let go.

Now be aware of your whole body, lying quiet and still.
As you breathe out, let go, and let your body sink gently into the
floor.

➤ Allow your breath to flow naturally. Let it take its own natural
course. With each outbreath, let go and feel your body sinking into
the floor. Allow your whole being to come to rest.

➤ Lie still for a few minutes, or for whatever time you have available,
enjoying the stillness.

➤ When you are ready to get up, take time to make the transition between stillness and movement.

➤ First, become aware of your five senses.

➤ Become aware of the the sense of *touch* – the contact of the body with the floor.

➤ Become aware of the sense of *taste* – swallow gently and become aware of the taste in the mouth.

➤ Become aware of the sense of *smell* as you begin to breathe more deeply.

➤ Become aware of the sense of *hearing* – the sounds all around you.

➤ Become aware of the sense of sight – the darkness behind your closed eyes.

➤ Become aware of the space your body is lying in, and of the space all around your body.

➤ Become aware of your surroundings.

➤ Then begin to move, first gently curling and stretching your fingers and toes.

➤ Have a good stretch, and then bring your knees to your abdomen. Hug yourself, and rock gently from side to side.

➤ Roll over onto one side and when you feel ready to sit up, ease yourself up gently into a sitting position.

➤ Sit quietly for a few moments, observing your breath.

The progression through the body is simple and straightforward, and you will probably find that you can remember it after you have practised it a few times. You really only need to remember the order of body parts, to breathe in as you bring your attention to each one, and to let go as you breathe out:

Feet	*Hands*
Shins	*Forearms*
Kneecaps	*Upper arms*
Thighs	*Throat*
Abdomen	*Back of the head*
Solar plexus	*Jaw*
Upper chest	*Eyes*
Spine	*Scalp*

At first, I suggest you keep to one breath for each part of the body. Then, if you have the time for a longer practice, you can let your attention rest at each point for two or three or more breaths, letting go with each outbreath.

In the beginning you may find it helpful to have the instructions read out to you. You could record them on a tape, or ask someone you trust and whose voice you love to do this for you. The instructions should be read slowly, with pauses to allow you time to experience the effects of the practice. Alternatively, you may wish to send for the tape that has been made to accompany this book.

When you have used the tape for a while you will be able to put it aside and do the practice on your own.

In sitting still and rest shall you be saved
In quietness and confidence shall be your strength.
                                                    Isaiah

If you would like a copy of the audio cassette tape that has been made to accompany this chapter and the previous chapter on breathing, please write, enclosing a cheque or postal order for £7.50 (£8.50 outside the U.K.), to Julie Friedeberger, c/o Element Books Ltd, Longmead, Shaftesbury, Dorset SP7 8PL.

10   Regaining Movement after Breast Surgery

During the first, relatively brief post-operative stage of coming to terms with breast cancer I was preoccupied with my physical recuperation to the exclusion of everything else. I had closed my mind to all the more serious, long-term implications of the disease, and had no idea how much work I would soon be having to do on all the other levels. All I could think about was getting back the full use of my arm and shoulder. I laughed at myself when I realized how I had been blinkering myself despite my good intentions not to; later I came to see how useful that had been as a delaying tactic. With my mind fixed on the first essential physical task, I was protected from grappling with the emotional issues I wasn't yet ready to face.

Which was just as well. As Swamiji pointed out, if I had had to cope with everything at once, the process of physical recovery would have taken longer and been harder. One thing, one stage at a time.

The day after he did my mastectomy, Alan Stoker came to check on me. 'I hope you aren't too uncomfortable?' he asked. I admitted that I didn't feel much like moving my left arm. 'Do move it,' he said. 'Move it as soon and as much as possible. If you don't, your shoulder will stiffen up.'

Afterwards, speaking to women who weren't given that good advice, whose scars began to pull and tighten after a week or two, and who are now having to put up with chronic stiffness, discomfort and restriction of their arm and shoulder movement, I realized even more how important post-operative wound management is, how essential it is to start moving as soon as possible after surgery, and to keep moving. And to do the right kind of exercises in the right way in order to restore full movement and strength and elasticity to the entire operated area.

Breast surgery, whether conservative or radical, is external and therefore relatively straightforward. Apart from the risks accompanying a general anaesthetic (fewer now than in the past) it is considered to be a very safe operation. But it can have extensive after-effects, some of them lasting, particularly if the axillary lymph nodes have also been removed.

After my mastectomy, my left armpit and the left side of my chest and ribcage were rock-hard and completely inelastic. My arm and shoulder movement were very restricted. For what seemed an eternity (though in fact was only a few weeks) the entire area felt as though it would never work properly again. But it did. Six weeks after surgery I could move, stretch, lift and drive as well as ever, and was able to return to doing the yoga postures I love.

The whole area was also totally numb. It still is, and apparently it always will be, because the second thoracic nerve which supplies it was severed. It feels odd, but it isn't painful or unpleasant, and I have got used to it. It doesn't stop me doing anything. And I am not altogether sorry to be left with this tenacious bit of sensory evidence that I am not the same as I was before. It's a reminder, and I do not want to forget I have had breast cancer.

Alan Stoker has since told me that this isn't routinely done; surgeons try to preserve the nerve if they can, but if it traverses very close to the lymph nodes that are to be cut out, it may have to be be removed with them.

As soon as I got out of hospital, where the physiotherapy had been perfunctory, I asked Alan Thompson to recommend someone, and that was how I met Zena Schofield. Zena is a manipulation physiotherapist, and the work she did with me got my arm fully functioning again more quickly than I had thought possible. It was hard work, but progress was rapid and steady. Each time I saw Zena she stretched me a little further than before, and this always gave me a new point to move on from. She gave me exercises to do at home: each time, I went away with something new to practise, with noticeable results at our next session. She was wonderfully supportive, as interested in the problem as I was and as enthusiastic about cracking it. The whole process was rewarding and thoroughly enjoyable, and I learned a great deal about the functioning of the pectoral muscles which I have since been able to integrate into my teaching. By the end of January the job was done.[16]

After breast surgery, regaining full arm and shoulder movement takes time and patient effort, particularly if the operation also involved lymph node clearance. The restriction on movement is mainly due to the bruising of the pectoral major muscles, which underlie the breast and stretch from the breastbone and collarbone to the upper arm, and the pectoral minor muscles in the armpit. If any muscle tissue has been cut during surgery there will be some weakness, and this too will take time to overcome.

A friend of a friend, who had had surgery for breast cancer several years earlier, told me that it is standard practice when removing the axillary nodes to cut the pectoral minor muscle, but that it isn't absolutely necessary to do so. She hadn't known about this, her muscle had been cut, and it had taken her three years to regain full strength in her arm. This was as serious a hindrance to her work as a potter as it would have been to mine as a yoga teacher. When I asked Alan Stoker about it he said that it was customary to cut the muscle because it gave them the clearest passage if they were doing a complete axillary clearance, but that he could manage without, and promised that he would. And he did. The first thing he said to me when he came to see me after the operation was 'Your muscles are intact.' As a result I suffered no weakness, which would have taken much longer to overcome than the stiffness.

The task of regaining movement may seem daunting. Your arm and shoulder hurt, and you don't want to do anything to make them hurt more. You may not want to move at all. You may feel nervous about your stitches and, while you're still in hospital, your drains. You may be horrified when you look at your wound; you may not want to look at it or think about it. You may want to pretend the whole thing never happened, and that may stop you paying proper attention to it. But if you don't start moving, and keep moving, you will stiffen up.

In hospital, you may or may not be given useful help. A physiotherapist came to see me only after I asked; she spent ten minutes with me, showed me one exercise, and told me that full movement would come back as soon as the drains came out. This proved, discouragingly but not surprisingly, to be wildly mistaken.

My experience may not have been typical, but I know women whose experience was similar or worse. One friend was told nothing, and was given no suitable exercises. Three years on, her movement is restricted and her scar is tight, dry and painful. One of my students, whose mastectomy was performed three years before she started yoga, suffered severe discomfort and movement restriction which took another three years of patient effort to overcome.

But I have heard happier stories too: hospital physiotherapy departments no doubt vary widely. The point is that if you are not given adequate specialist help in hospital, you may need to seek effective guidance independently. Where recovery from a major operation is concerned, we need to do all we can to aid it, even to the extent of paying for skilled private care, to which we might normally give a low priority.

Your movement won't come back by itself. Without help, or strong motivation to work on yourself, or both, you may stiffen up and be left with permanent tightness and adhesions. It can then take years to undo the damage, and it may not be possible to undo it completely. This is both unfortunate and unnecessary. Unless there are unforeseen complications to surgery, six to eight weeks of regular exercise of the right kind can fully restore movement and elasticity to their pre-operation state.

There is a great deal you can do to help yourself. For a start you need to exercise regularly. Little and often is best: short periods of five or ten minutes, a few times a day. The exercises need to be targeted precisely to the area affected by the surgery. Ordinary keep-fit stretches, and even most yoga postures, are not specific enough, though it will be good for you to keep doing what you like to do, as long as it doesn't overtire you. Swimming is excellent. I was off to the local pool as soon as my wound was healed, and the breast stroke I normally use really stretched out my pectoral muscles and armpit and my scar. Side stroke and back stroke were effective too.

What will probably be more helpful than anything else is some sessions with a good physiotherapist. The support and encouragement I had from Zena kept my nose enthusiastically to the grindstone and was as helpful in the overall healing process as the exercises she taught me.

Six exercises were particularly helpful. They are based on some of those that Zena gave me, which I have adapted a little. The main difference is the integration of the yoga technique of co-ordinating movement with breath. This helps you to soften and relax into the stretches, which makes them more effective.

First, here is some general guidance on what your objective is and how to proceed. Your movement is at present restricted; to what degree depends on the kind and extent of the surgery you have had, the skill with which it was performed, and your age, general physical condition and level of fitness before surgery. Whatever combination of these factors applies, your aim is to progress from your present restricted state to the restoration of full elasticity of the muscles and full-range movement of the arm and the shoulder joint, and this should be possible within a reasonable time, if you exercise regularly and correctly.

If you always exercise within your existing range of movement, stopping whenever you begin to feel discomfort, you'll get 'stuck' and you won't improve. At the other extreme, if you are over-enthusiastic, and force movements beyond discomfort into severe pain, you may damage your already bruised soft tissues.

You need to find a balance between working too strongly and working too gently, but bear in mind that you do need to push yourself a little, and that this will sometimes cause discomfort.

Physical sensations are difficult to describe, and we all experience them differently; the words 'discomfort' and 'pain' mean different things to different people, and one person's discomfort may be another person's pain. It isn't easy, therefore, to give ground rules that will suit everyone, or even convey the same meaning to everyone.

If you are a fit, active, person, highly motivated to succeed and inclined to push yourself too hard, I don't want to encourage you to push yourself harder: asking *you* to tolerate a little 'pain' might make you carry on through the pain barrier till it really hurts! You need to be careful, and self-aware. The exercises are meant to *aid* the healing process, not hinder it. Please don't push yourself too hard, too fast.

On the other hand, if you are more laid back and not generally inclined to challenge yourself, my asking you to tolerate some 'discomfort' might encourage you to stop before you've made any progress.

Zena used the word 'nudge' for what she wanted me to do, and that worked for me. If you work slowly and mindfully, and keep 'nudging' each movement a bit beyond discomfort to the point where it starts to feel just a little painful, you should make steady progress without doing yourself any damage.

Note: If you are unsure about the suitability of any of the following exercises for you, please consult your doctor or physiotherapist. If in doubt, omit it.

Three standing exercises

These three exercises can be done at any time, at odd moments during the day (while you're waiting for the kettle to boil, for example). Exercises 2 and 3 are equally good for stretching the pectoral muscles on the other side, so practise them on both sides.

1 Stand facing a wall, and rest your chest and nose against it.

➤ Starting with your elbows bent and your hands alongside your face, gently 'walk' your fingertips up the wall. See figure 15.

Figure 15

➤ Keep your arms parallel, in line with your shoulders. 'Walk' to just past the point where you start to feel pain. Don't force it further, but do get to that point and a little beyond it. See figure 16.

Figure 16

➤ Then walk your fingers back down the wall.

➤ Rest, and repeat the exercise a few more times.

➤ You can monitor your progress by pencil-marking the point you reach once a week.

2 Move away from the wall for this exercise, in which you are going to make big circles with your arm, to work the armpit and chest muscles on the operated side, fully rotate your shoulder, and stretch along the line of your scar.

➤ Start with your arms by your sides. Take your weak arm across the front of your body and stretch it up, round and back in a big arc, keeping it straight and turning it out from the shoulder so your thumb points back. See figures 17 and 18.

Figure 17   *Figure 18*

➤ Do this slowly. Feel the stretch along your pectoral muscles and your scar line, and feel your armpit opening. Don't overstretch, but do take it a little further than is comfortable.

➤ Circle your arm all the way down and round to your starting point. When it's about at shoulder level, start turning it from the shoulder the other way (a full rotation of the arm in the shoulder joint). As you bring the arm round in front, your thumb will be pointing down and your palm will face forward.

Breathing: **in** *as you bring the arm across and up,* **out** *as you bring it down and round in front.*

3 In this exercise you'll be working on opening your armpit and stretching your pectoral muscles and along your scar line, more strongly this time.

➤ Stand side-on to the wall (operated side first), about 18 inches (45cm) away from it.

➤ Take your arm across and up as in exercise 1, rotating it from the shoulder so your thumb points back.

➤ Rest the palm of your hand, from heel to fingertips, against the wall, a little higher than your shoulder. Experience this stretch for a few moments, breathing naturally. See figure 19.

Figure 19

➤ This first step is in itself quite a strong stretch, so introduce the extensions gradually.

➤ *Extension 1* Take a step forward and feel the stronger stretch.

➤ *Extension 2* Turn your trunk and head away from the wall and feel the increased stretch. Take the stretch to just beyond the point of discomfort. See figure 20.

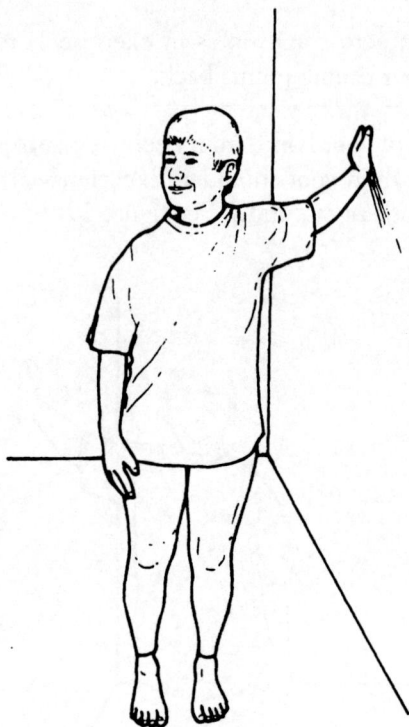

Figure 20

➤ Release the stretch by turning your trunk and head to the front. Do this several times – five at first, increasing to ten or more. Release your arm gently.

*Breathing: natural breathing in the first stage and extension 1. In extension 2 breathe **out** as you turn your trunk and head, **in** as you return to the starting position.*

Three exercises on the floor

4 Here, grasping a walking stick or broom handle with both hands enables your strong arm to support your weaker arm.

➤ Rest the stick on your abdomen and grasp it firmly with both hands, shoulder-width apart. See figure 21.

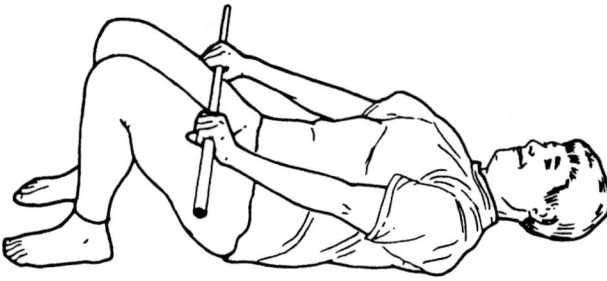

Figure 21

➤ Straighten your arms. Raise the stick, keeping your arms straight. Stretch your arms up towards the ceiling and back behind your head.

➤ Keep your lower back in contact with the floor: don't let it come up.

➤ Bring your hands and the stick as close to the floor behind you as you can comfortably, and just a little further, nudging just past the point where it starts to hurt a little, but without forcing. See Figure 22.

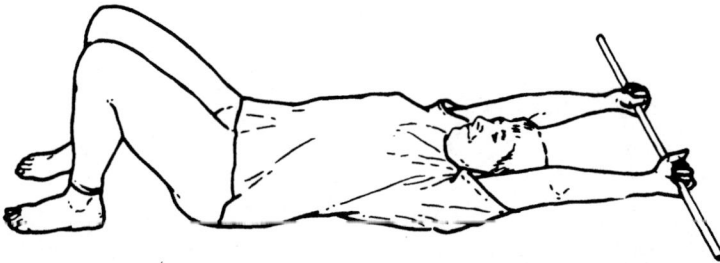

Figure 22

➤ Then lift the stick and return it to the starting position, keeping your arms straight.

➤ Repeat this several times, gradually increasing the number of repetitions.

Breathing: **in** *as you take the stick back overhead,* **out** *as you return it to the starting position.*

5 Lie with a comfortable pillow under your head, and rest your head in your clasped hands.

➤ Lift your elbows up around your face. See figure 23.

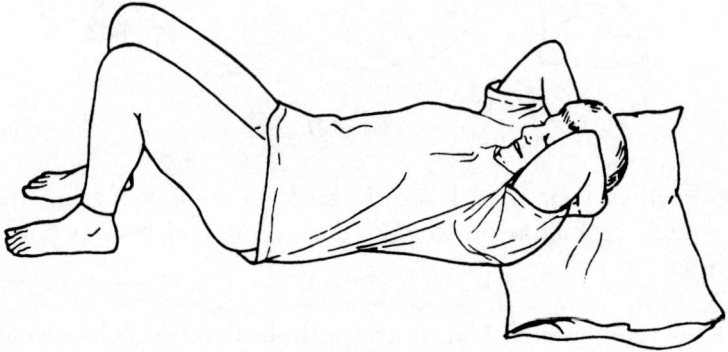

Figure 23

➤ Then lower them slowly and gently, with a feeling of opening and releasing through chest and armpits. See figure 24.

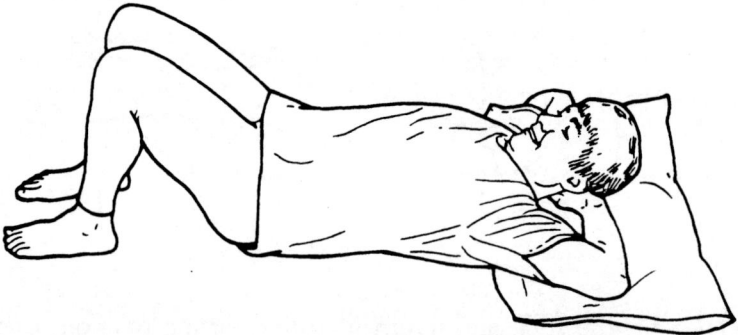

Figure 24

➤ Don't force the stretch. Hold it for a moment at the point of discomfort, then 'nudge' it a little further, pressing your elbows into the pillow.

➤ Repeat this several times.

➤ You may need two pillows at first. As you improve you can remove one of them, and when your chest and armpit open fully and your elbows sink easily all the way to the floor, remove the other.

Breathing: **in** *as you raise your elbows,* **out** *as you lower and press them down.*

6 Here is a simple exercise to help you open and stretch through your armpits, improve the elasticity of your pectoral and intercostal muscles, and stretch along the line of your scar. It should be left until you have practised the others and have already regained some of the stretchiness in the pectoral muscles: see the note below.

➤ Lie with your knees bent and your arms resting alongside your body, palms on the floor. Breathing in, raise both arms and take them back behind you, as far as you can without straining.

➤ Your arm and hand on the operated side will be further from the floor than the other: don't try to force them down.

➤ Breathing out, relax both your arms, letting your elbows bend until they touch the floor. The whole surface of both arms should be resting on the floor, if possible. See figure 25.

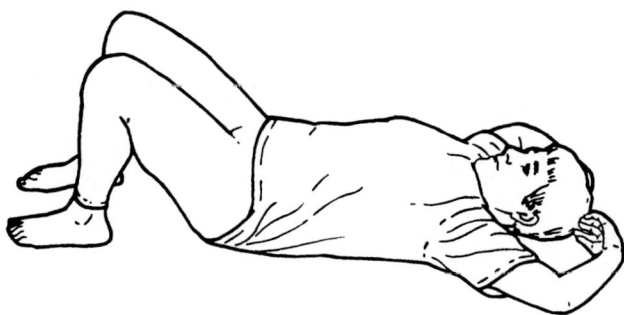

Figure 25

Note: If your elbow on the operated side does not reach the floor in the first few weeks after surgery, leave this exercise till after you have made some progress with the others.

➤ Inhale as you slide your elbow gently back along the floor, keeping it in contact with the floor. See figure 26.

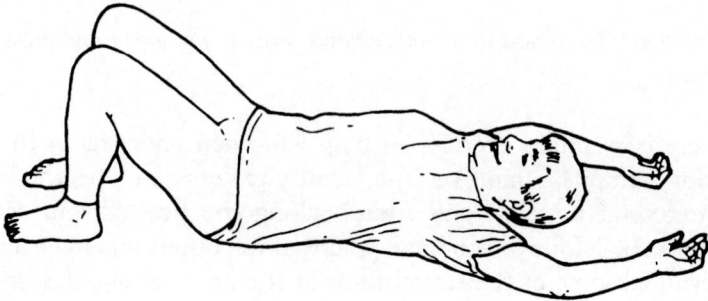

Figure 26

➤ Keep your arm, hand and fingers soft and relaxed. They aren't doing anything; the stretch is through the armpit, chest and ribcage.

➤ Exhale as you release the stretch and allow your elbow to slide back to its starting point.

➤ Don't try to 'get anywhere'. Your elbow may move back only a little way. That's fine. Remember that your arm and hand aren't meant to be working: keep them relaxed and passive in order to get the maximum stretch through the armpit, ribcage and chest. This is where you should feel it.

➤ Do this several times on the operated side, and then give your other side a turn. Then do the movement with both arms together.

➤ If your arms get tired, do give them a rest in between.

*Breathing: in as you stretch, **out** as you release.*

I think you'll find all these exercises effective for stretching tight pectoral muscles and opening up tight armpits. (Muscles and armpits that haven't had surgery can benefit from them too – most of us are a bit tight in this area!) If you start them as soon as possible after surgery, and continue to do them regularly, you will soon restore your movement and your capacity to stretch to what it was before surgery, and perhaps even beyond that.

Not all mastectomies are performed in the same way. My own scar, 9 inches (22cm) long, runs diagonally from the middle of my sternum to the top of my left armpit. Most of the exercises will still be suitable if your scar is different, but one or two may need to be modified, and if any is not suitable for you, omit it and follow the advice of your physiotherapist.

Caring for your scar

Scar tissue goes on forming for a full year (some say two years) after surgery, and to avoid adhesions and permanent tightness, you need to keep working at your stretching exercises all through that first year.

I did mine diligently for the first three months. Then I slackened off occasionally, and it would take only two or three days for the scar to start feeling tight. Two years on, I am still very aware of the area and of the need to keep it stretched out.

Once your wound has healed you can start massaging the scar (unless you are having radiotherapy, in which case you should ask your radiologist when you can safely use creams or oils on the scar and surrounding skin.) Any good quality, fairly rich cream will be helpful, but you might like to try the following recipe for the mixture of essential oils Swamiji gave me, which I've found very pleasant and effective.

> 3 drops myrrh (good for the skin), and
> 5 drops lavender (cleansing and healing).

Dissolve these (shake well) in 10ml of a carrier oil, such as almond oil. You can prepare larger quantities of the mixture: just keep the ratio the same (for example, 15 drops myrrh and 25 lavender to 50 mls almond oil).

Massaging the oil or cream into the scar and surrounding skin two or three times a day will help prevent adhesions and the pulling sensations, dryness and tightness that many women experience. It will also keep the scar soft and smooth, silky and supple.

When massaging, use firm, vigorous finger pressure, fairly deep. Don't just do 'skin-polishing', but dig in. Work back and forth, and in a circular motion, moving the scar against the underlying tissue. Keep working along the scar without lingering too long on any one area. Pay extra attention to any especially tight or puckered areas. While massaging, use your other thumb and forefinger to stretch along the scar line. Or you can combine your massage with exercise 3, with your arm outstretched and your hand on the wall behind you.

Stretching and massaging both speed healing by stimulating blood circulation to the area. Another (very invigorating!) way to do this is to spray the scar with cold water for 30 seconds or so after a bath or shower.

Stretching and massaging are important for another reason. You have had an enormous shock to your entire system, emotionally and mentally as well as physically. Your body has been cut, and you've lost a part of it. You've suffered a wound. For a while, you may feel cut off from that numb, painful, irrevocably altered area. You may feel it isn't part of you any more; that you don't even want it to be part of you. You may not want to look at it or touch it. These feelings are natural. But your wound is a part of you. Don't reject it, meet it lovingly; make friends with it, care for it tenderly, as you would care for a baby or a child. You need to reclaim that injured part of you, welcome it, re-integrate it into yourself. For this to happen, you need to look at your wound, and touch it, often and gently and with kindness and love.

Stretching and massaging will help not only your physical healing. It will encourage your deeper healing by letting you feel you are nurturing the bruised, altered area of your body, and helping you let go of any squeamish, anxious or angry feelings you may be having about it. It will help you reclaim and accept it as a lovable part of you: different now, but all right.

Know ye not that ye are the temple of God,
and the Spirit of God dwelleth in you?
                St Paul: Corinthians

Epilogue
'All Shall Be Well'

All shall be well, and all shall will be well, and all manner of thing shall be well.

Julian of Norwich

As I write this, it's two years since I discovered my lump and nearly one year since I finished writing the main body of *A Visible Wound*. The process of assimilating the experience of cancer and transcending the trauma of it is a long and ongoing one. Nevertheless, I've begun to feel that I've arrived at a point at which I can look back and say: 'I've come through.'

I know I've thought that before, and said it before, and been wrong; and I haven't forgotten that I described the process as the peeling of an onion, with another layer always awaiting you underneath the one you've just stripped off. It *is* just like that, so no doubt more layers await me. But I suspect that these are now more likely to be related to new circumstances and challenges: for example, a local recurrence would certainly give me a few new layers to get to grips with, and a metastatic recurrence – or the approach of death – a whole new onion to peel.

All this lies in the unknown, unforeseeable future, and while I don't ignore the possibilities, neither do I anticipate them. I do pay attention to them, so that if and when they happen they won't take me unawares, but they don't prey on my mind or affect my work or cloud my life. I think I've come through.

Even if I weren't pretty sure of this in myself, I would be able to infer it from my journal. It is no longer all about cancer. I use it now for anything I want to understand and gain clarity on, and it is as great a help as it has always been, but it is many months since I needed it to help me deal with cancer and its issues.

A Visible Wound has been about my coming through the experience of breast cancer and mastectomy surgery, and about everything that helped me come through. I hope it will give others help, both spiritual and practical, as they work their own way through. This Epilogue, though it may not be the end of the story, is an 'interim conclusion', bringing the reader abreast of where the journey has taken me since early 1995 when I 'finished' the book. It is also a summation, recapitulating and uniting its main themes.

I could not have written the book without all the help I have been given on my journey through cancer. In that help I was truly blessed, and I know it. I am deeply thankful to Klaus and Swamiji for their love and their guidance, to Alan Stoker for his skill, kindness, encouragement and honesty, to my students and friends for the help they gave for as long as it was needed, and to all of them for their healing presence in my life. It is no reflection on their contribution to my healing for me to say – and I say it for the sake of my readers – that I think I made it easier for them to help me by being open to their help, and letting them know that I needed them.

Many women go through breast cancer without the wealth of sustaining love and support that I have had. But that makes it even more important for us to get the help we need wherever we can. And so I make an appeal to all who find themselves facing a cancer diagnosis, indeed to anyone, woman or man, facing the crisis of any serious illness: acknowledge your need for help. Identify the people and sources from which the help you need and could accept might come. Ask for help, and be open to the help that is offered.

It is so difficult for some of us to ask for help, to accept help. We may be the one who is always there to give support to others; or perhaps we shrink from 'bothering' our friends with our own concerns. Perhaps we make light of our troubles in order to spare others or reassure ourselves. 'I'm fine,' we say, when asked how we are, 'mustn't grumble'.

But try to remember the affirmation *'It's my turn to practise the generosity of receiving.'* Be generous to your friends. They will want to help, and some of them will actually be able to, with practical things like shopping and child care and housework, and accompanying you on hospital visits. But they may not find it easy to offer help unless you ask. The 'flip side' of our general reluctance to request help is the hesitancy so many of us feel about approaching others who are ill or bereaved: we may be sympathetic, we may even be grieving for them, but we fear to intrude. Asking for help dissolves that fear, and makes it possible for help to be given.

But there is, of course, a widespread fear of cancer, which one person in three can expect to develop in the course of a lifetime. Coming close to a person with cancer can trigger that fear, and not everyone can cope with it; so you have to expect some disappointments. Don't let this deter you from asking, and don't be afraid of rejection. If you look you will also find generosity and kindness, sensitivity and love, often where you might have expected it least. If you allow yourself to be open to the healing help that is all around you, you may find one or two people (they won't necessarily be your closest friends) who can give you their time, listen to you, bear witness to your fear, pain and confusion, and empathize without feeling they have to 'fix' things for you, without giving advice or reassuring you that 'everything will be all right'.

'When you know you need help you have to ask for it, *really* ask,' my friend Shraddha said in her letter to me shortly after I was diagnosed. (Only a year later I was saying it back to her, when she got breast cancer and had to have a breast removed.) Of course that statement applies to asking friends for help. But that wasn't entirely what Shraddha meant by it. What she meant was prayer.

Before I had cancer, I had never really prayed. But in those early-morning vigils in my room, I did. I prayed for help. I opened my whole being to God's help, and I was helped.

Whether we 'believe in God' or not isn't an issue. Whatever our beliefs, even if we define ourselves as atheist, we can open ourselves and ask for help, for mercy. And if we really ask, help will come. Perhaps someone we don't know very well appears at our side and sticks to us through it all and becomes a friend; or we are given a book that throws light on what has happened to us, or a remark is made that opens our eyes to a new way of perceiving its meaning.

My help came in all these ways, and more. But the determining help came from the depths of my being, in the form of an answer to all my pleading, anguished questions about 'why' I had been dealt such an unfair, terrible blow.

I've described the moment in which I surrendered to the experience of cancer, the moment in which I knew that it had been given to me to learn from, and knew that I would go through it and live and emerge on the other side of it transformed and healed. In that moment, I stopped kicking, did a 180-degree turn, and began to look cancer and death in the face. Not for a day since has the knowledge given me in that moment left me. It was the beginning of transformation, and, I believe, the most significant factor in my healing.

In that same moment I also knew that 'my' own strength was not going to be enough to get me through, but that there was another strength behind me that I could trust absolutely. I had a sense of release, of lying back, letting go of struggle, and being borne along on a strong tide. From that moment on, it was steady sailing.

I never felt that being given that blessing, that grace, for that was what it was, absolved me from my own responsibilities: to my students, to all the people I loved, to my illness, and to myself and the journey I had to make. That whole journey still lay ahead of me, the journey from grief and fear and anger, to acknowledgement and acceptance and healing, and I had to take responsibility for it. Whatever was being done, God was doing it and I was just helping, but my job was to be a good helper. My trust in that Power behind me, and in my new and growing understanding of illness, became the tide to ride, on the journey.

I have said, often, that I think it is vital for anyone with cancer to allow time for true healing – not just physical recovery – to take place.

I was lucky. I had people around me who could take over my responsibilities so that I was under no pressure to return to them until I was ready to, and I gave myself the time that was needed for the healing process to get well underway. That turned out to be five months: not a particularly long time. For someone else it might be six, or ten or more. For some it might only be three or four. Whatever the length of time needed, it is essential to the healing process and it should be taken.

So here is another appeal, to all women (and men) with cancer. Take time. Give yourself the time to heal, the time for self-discovery. Please don't think 'I've got to get over this and get back to work quickly and forget it ever happened.' Of course I realize that some women, especially working women and mothers with young children, will not find this easy. But if it can possibly be done (perhaps with the help of work colleagues who can take over for a while, or of partners or older children who can take more responsibility, or relatives, or friends, or neighbours) it should be done.

There really are secret miracles at work within us that only Time can bring forth – but we have got to be responsible for allowing Time the time to do its work.

Many, perhaps most, women feel guilty about taking time for themselves. Not being altogether an exception to the rule, I haven't got an easy answer to this one. But guilt is an obstacle to healing, and we need to find a way of overcoming it.

From my own experience I know how much it helps to have a partner to encourage you, so my appeal is made also to the partners and families of women with cancer. In your distress at seeing someone you love having to go through major surgery and perhaps unpleasant further treatment, it is natural to want the whole awful business to be over and done with as quickly as possible, and for your wife/partner/mother/lover to be all right again. But the best way of helping may be for you to understand the need for healing time, and to let her know that you understand it. Encourage her in every way that you can to allow herself the time she needs, and discourage her from feeling guilty about it.

Klaus had the knack of being able to put the brakes on whenever I got restive (which was fairly often!). Whenever I started muttering about malingering, he would say, calmly, 'What's the hurry, it's early days yet, take your time.' When I wondered out loud whether 'people' might be starting to think it was time I got off my bottom and got back to work, he simply said 'That doesn't arise.'

Instinctively he knew, even before I did, that though I had bounced back from surgery quickly, there was more to coming to terms with cancer than either of us were then consciously aware of. And he was able to witness and empathize with my fears, and my tears, without shutting himself off from them, or needing to rescue me from them with empty reassurance; without trying to make me (or himself) 'feel better'. He knew that what I was going through was all part of the healing process, and he was just *there* with me. We've shared the experience; it happened to us both, and we held onto each other through it.

When we talk about it now, or when I tell friends we haven't seen for a long time how good he was, he denies that there was anything special about what he did. But there was, and it was what I needed.

Breast cancer is a cataclysm that affects everyone close to us. Their response to it can have a considerable, even a decisive, effect on how we get through it. I've spoken about Klaus's role in my healing in the hope of inspiring other husbands, other lovers, to see what is truly helpful, and to try, in their own way, to do for their wives and lovers what Klaus was able to do for me.

Of course, everything I have said applies equally to *men* who have cancer and to their wives and partners.

How the healing time is used will, naturally, be decided by each individual, and each of us must find a method, a way through, that is right.

For me, there is no question that true healing is grounded in self-acceptance, and in acceptance of reality, of 'the thing as it is'; and that this begins with acknowledgement and acceptance of our emotions. It is vital that we not deny our fear, grief and anger, for in doing so we only waste our precious energy in repression. Only if we allow our feelings to surface, and really look at them, can we start to understand them, accept them, transcend the pain they give us, and emerge from their turmoil into clarity and true acceptance of ourselves as we are, of things as they are, of life as it is.

This understanding of how the therapeutic process works was at the heart of the method I used to work my way through. I found it necessary, essential, to look very closely at everything that came up for me during the healing process. In contemplation and reflection, through meditation and through journal-writing, I used those months, and the rest of the first year after I returned to teaching, to examine and explore all the feelings and thoughts that cancer gave rise to. Doing this has released me from their power and enabled me to let go of them. It has freed my energy for teaching, for writing, for living.

Yoga has sustained me on the journey, in two ways.

The basic breathing, relaxation and stretching techniques I've included in Chapters 8, 9 and 10 were a great help to me, and I hope that others will find them helpful as they go through their own healing process.

My outlook on life, my understanding of the therapeutic process, and the perspective I have gained on the issues that confront us when illness brings us face to face with the reality of death, are grounded in yoga philosophy and psychology. They have brought me through, and I hope I have succeeded in sharing them in a way that may give others useful insight.

The detachment I have spoken of has been an integral part of the process. Developing the detachment and discernment that enable us to examine and release our feelings instead of getting entangled in them is a technique: everyone can learn it. Once we understand that we don't *have* to get entangled, all that is needed is to let our feelings come up, and look at them, and own them. With practice, we learn how to do this. We may not have to do anything else. Clarity, insight and discrimination unfold from this process of observation, acknowledgement and acceptance. In this, the breathing exercises I've given, especially breath awareness, will help.

Keeping a journal may be a help to you, as it has been to me. My journal, which was born out of a desperate need to keep in touch with myself on the cancer roller-coaster, has become an essential part of my life. It is my guide and my friend. It helps me to be truthful with myself, to discover how I really feel and what I really think. Without the journal, which quickly became an unerringly sensitive tool for drawing out of myself whatever needed to be looked at, I would probably still be struggling with buried fears, would still be working through my feelings, would not have reached the knowledge and the peace of mind that lay beyond them. I would have done this work in any case, because I have always been naturally self-reflective and analytical, but without the journal it would have taken much longer.

And without the journal there would have been no book. Ailsa wrote to me recently after reading the manuscript that 'One of the gifts of cancer which you don't mention is that it has helped you to blossom as a writer.' That is true, and it is journal-keeping that has done it. So cancer and my journal have brought me, at 60, to my cherished childhood goal, abandoned for almost half a century: to 'be a writer when I grow up'. That *is* a gift!

But you don't have to 'be a writer' to keep a journal. Journal-keeping is a completely private undertaking. You are writing for yourself; no one else will see it unless you show it to them, and you shouldn't show it to anyone, for it's essential that you know you aren't trying to impress anyone, and that you don't have to worry about anyone judging what you write. There should be no 'audience' looking over your shoulder.

I've explained that journal-writing and meditation techniques have much in common: each opens the possibility of looking at whatever comes up, and reflecting on it without getting involved with it. Both practices develop detachment, and bring clarity, acceptance and peace.

My method was a kind of self-therapy, founded on my understanding of how emotions can be observed, dealt with and released, and it worked for me. With the help of the journal and of yoga and of my friends I was able to go through this process on my own. But the process is the same, and the method valid, whether we do it on our own or with the help of a qualified therapist or counsellor. As it happened, I didn't need professional help, but I would certainly have sought it if I had, and would certainly encourage others to seek it if the need for it is felt – with the proviso that it is important to find a therapist who has dealt with his or her own fear of death, and can listen to yours without trying to reassure you.

A word about support groups may also be appropriate here. They can be helpful, but be careful which one you choose, and don't feel you have to commit yourself to regular membership until you have attended a few sessions and are quite sure that you are comfortable with its members and the way it is run. There are many types and many stages of cancer. If you have just had treatment for early breast cancer, and are well on your way to recovery with a good prognosis, you may or may not find it useful to join a support group in which other women are grappling with the traumatic shock of metastatic recurrences or dealing with the approach of death. As when choosing any source of potential help, be sure it is what *you* need, what will help *you*.

The book had its title before I had even started to write it. From the moment that I knew I would write a book, I knew it would be called *A Visible Wound*. The reference was, then, merely to my physical wound: the loss of the breast, the scar, the firm hardness of my 'flat' side. The title embodied my wish, on the personal and professional levels, to be truthful about what I am, a single-breasted woman. It reflected my wish, on the political level, to dissociate myself from the conspiracy of denial and silence that surrounds breast cancer, to declare myself a warrior in the fight against it.

Continuing exploration and reflection in the time that has passed since then have revealed a still deeper significance of my visible wound. I have come to see the physical wound, the scar, as the outward manifestion of my inner journey. I am grateful to the friend who gave me the metaphor that expresses this truth of which I was aware, but had not found the words for, by suggesting that the surgeon's scalpel had opened the way in for me, leaving me with the symbol of that opening, the wound. The wearing of a false breast would have been, as I realized early on, a concealment of the physical reality, but it would also, more importantly, have been a closing of the opening, a denial of the journey itself, and of the self-knowledge and self-acceptance that have been the rewards of the journey.

> *To each is given a bag of tools,*
> *An hour glass, a book of rules*
> *And each must build, ere time has flown,*
> *A stumbling block, a stepping stone.*
> (source unknown)

Through having cancer I've learned that illness can be regarded, and used, not as an enemy to be fought or a catastrophic nuisance to be got over with and forgotten as quickly as possible, but as a precious, unique opportunity for spiritual growth, transformation and healing. It has been so for me, and I believe with all my heart that it can be so for all of us. We can, if we so choose, transform the stumbling block of illness into a stepping stone to healing and a fuller, richer, more useful life, a life in which we can put whatever we have learned, whatever we have become through the alchemy of our own transformation, at the service of others.

Now, two years on from breast cancer surgery, I am well. I have a peace, a strength, a firmer stability and a confidence that I did not have before. They are rooted in healing: in the deeper knowledge, and in the liberation from fear and from the striving for perfection, that cancer has given me.

I think of the Native American chant:

Cauldron of changes, feather on the bone
Arc of eternity, ring on the stone.
We are the old people
We are the new people
We are the same people
Wiser than before.

I remain alert to the possibility that cancer can and does recur; that my story does not end with the ending of this book. But I am, truly, not afraid. I have never forgotten what Swamiji said so emphatically, when my fears started to surface: 'You're clear *now*. If you get a recurrence in however many years' time, you'll deal with it *then*.'

I know now that I can and will deal with it if and when it happens. I hope it won't happen for a very long time. But I'm prepared. I am fully back in the swing of my life, teaching, writing, planning a new teacher-training course. I love my work. I am happy with my life as it is. I look forward to the remaining years of it, whatever their number, trusting that whatever happens to me will not exceed my capacity to deal with it.

And I look back on the last two years with wonder at all that has happened, and gratitude for all I have been given. If I had been asked,

I would not have chosen to have cancer. But I have had cancer, and it has changed my life, and I would on no account have missed the experience, which has taught me so much.

Nevertheless, illness and death are part of life, and it helps me to keep looking at them. Sogyal Rinpoche's flat statment, 'Death is simply a fact of life', entered my consciousness six weeks or so after surgery when my fears of recurrence and death began to surface. At about the same time I admitted my fears to Alan Stoker, who did not reassure me as I had half hoped he would, but simply said 'These are facts of life, and you have to learn to accept them.'

So I started looking at them, and it took time, but I did accept them.

The acceptance that I have arrived at through having cancer, through surrendering to it instead of struggling against it, through looking at illness and death and getting some real understanding of them, through acknowledging death as a fact of life, has freed me, to a considerable extent, from fear of death.

It may not have freed me entirely – how can I know, until the time arrives for me to go? But the freedom and knowledge that I do have are great gifts, and I don't want them to slip away from me now that I am well. So I keep on looking. I keep, I suppose you could say, a steady eye on the ball.

And with Julian of Norwich I trust that – whatever happens – all shall be well.

Practical Matters

In Britain, according to the latest available figures there are more than 30,000 new cases of breast cancer every year, and about 15,000 deaths. Britain's death rate from breast cancer is the highest in the world, and its five-year survival rate is one of the lowest. In the United States 182,000 new cases are diagnosed and there are 46,000 deaths.

One in 12 women in Britain can expect to develop breast cancer in the course of her lifetime. In the United States the rate is 1 in 10. In Canada it is 1 in 13; in Australia 1 in 16; in New Zealand 1 in 14.[17]

In the developing countries, where there is little money for proper treatment, the situation is graver still. Breast cancer is a vicious epidemic, and the money and effort ploughed by the richer countries into sophisticated technology, chemical warfare on cancer, screening and research into possible cures have not improved the statistics. They are getting worse, not better.

Certainly, it is time to start looking seriously into the causes of breast cancer, time to start concentrating on prevention, and this, as I have already said, is a political issue.

In the United States some progress appears to have been made on the political front. In Britain, we are still waiting for our government to absorb this message, and for our health care system to end the lottery that is breast cancer treatment. But while we wait for research to be done – and acted upon – into breast cancer's causes, every woman should be aware that it can happen to any of us.

Many factors influence whether a woman develops breast cancer: personal, genetic and hereditary, social and sexual, environmental and nutritional. Some of these may be under our individual control, some may not. But one thing is certain, and *is* under our control. Early detection has a bearing on the future course of the disease in a high proportion of cases. Women whose breast cancers are discovered and treated early have a much better chance of long-term survival without recurrence.

So: examine your breasts regularly, and take advantage of regular screening if you are offered it.

Women who have already had breast cancer may think it a bit late in the day to be talking about breast self-examination. But we who have had it need to be aware that we are the ones most at risk of developing cancer in the other breast, so the following notes apply to us all.

➤ Be aware of your breast(s) and get to know their normal feel and appearance. If you discover a lump, go to your doctor immediately. Don't panic, but *go*. A very high proportion of lumps turns out to be non-malignant, but if you get one that is, the sooner it is found and dealt with the better.

➤ Other warning signs to look out for are a dent, dimple or change in the size or shape of the breast; a change in the position of a nipple or an unfamiliar discharge or bleeding from it; any puckering of the skin or change in its texture.

➤ Doctors sometimes make mistakes. The individual doctor may see many patients with breast lumps, but only one or two a year whose lumps are breast cancer; not enough always to be able to distinguish them accurately. Referral for specialist investigation may be called for, but some doctors may fear getting a reputation for 'crying wolf' if they make too many referrals. Older practitioners may not always be aware of current research and trends in the disease: for example, breast cancer has always been considered a disease of middle and old age, and the risk does increase with age, but increasing numbers of women are now developing it in their twenties and thirties. Young women's lumps are not always benign, but young women are too often told 'There's nothing to worry about at your age.'

➤ There has been no shortage of reports about delays in referring women with clear symptoms to specialists. There is a real danger here. Because it is natural to want to be relieved of anxiety, it is easy to accept reassurance. If your symptoms are still there after a short time (weeks, not months) go back to your doctor and insist on being referred for tests and examination, and make it clear that you want to see a breast cancer specialist.

➤ These remarks may be thought unfair to doctors, but it has to be recognized that unnecessary deaths have occurred because women have been reassured that their lumps or other symptoms were harmless when they were not. Death by delay should not happen: surely it is better to be safe than sorry.

➤ The mammogram (breast X-ray) is not an entirely reliable means of establishing whether or not a malignancy exists, particularly in younger women whose breast tissue is denser than that of post-menopausal women. Tumours do not always show up on these X-rays, which is one reason why screening by mammography for women under the age of 50 is not regarded as useful. A needle biopsy, a simple out-patient procedure performed under local anaesthetic, offers greater certainty. If you are not offered a biopsy, you should ask why.

➤ Women aged 50-64 in Britain are now offered a three-yearly mammogram under the national screening programme which began in 1990. There are two things to say about this. The first and most obvious is *go*. An enormous number of women offered screening don't go, for fear that something might be found. If something is there, the sooner it is found the better the outlook. Second, don't rely on the mammogram for a sense of security: continue with self-examination. Three-yearly screening may be better than none, but recent research has shown that it is not frequent enough; there is a fairly high incidence of missed cancers and interval cancers. I was one of these interval cases: I discovered my lump nearly two years after a negative screen.

➤ Before your appointments with your consultant or the registrar, make a list of your questions, and ask them. Don't be afraid of taking too much of their time: it's your life, your health. Most consultants will tell you what you want to know, but they wait for you to ask. This is only partly due to the pressure they are under; I think they genuinely try to be careful not to swamp people with any more information than they can take in at any one time. Your questions show that you have already thought of certain possibilities yourself, and that you may be able to take the answers on board.

➤ If you don't understand something your consultant says, ask for it to be explained again.

➤ Make sure someone, a partner or a friend, goes with you to every appointment. This is always helpful, and if you are given upsetting news it's essential to have someone with you. Your companion can talk everything over with you afterwards, and remind you of anything you couldn't or didn't take in, or have forgotten.

➤ It is difficult to remember everything that is said during a consultation, especially when you are anxious and frightened. Ask your companion to take notes for you. Better still, take a small cassette recorder with you and record the discussion for later listening (ask your consultant if this is acceptable before you switch on, though).

➤ If your diagnosis is positive, and surgery including clearance of the axillary lymph nodes is suggested, you should be aware that it is quite common for the pectoral minor muscle to be cut, and sometimes removed altogether. Although it is regarded as a relatively unimportant muscle, its removal causes weakness and prolongs the process of regaining strength and mobility. It may not always be necessary to cut the muscle, however. It's certainly worth asking.

➤ Surgery may mean a hospital stay of just a few days, but you could be in for a week or more if the lymph nodes are removed (this is because drainage takes longer, and the time varies with the individual). You'll be sleeping on your back at night, and you might get to feel a bit stiff and sore. This is why it's a good idea to get up and move around as much as possible during the day, as soon as you feel up to it.

➤ But even in bed you can be active! Here are a few 'bed exercises' for you to do during this time (and when you get home, too). You won't be able to do any movements involving the trunk and spine for awhile, but these will work the other joints of the body, stimulate your circulation, and get energy flowing. As they also speed the removal of toxins from the body, they may help you get over the effects of the anaesthetic quicker.

Do the exercises lying on your back, as often as you want to. Do them gently, don't tire yourself, and if any exercise for any reason doesn't feel right to you, please omit it.

Fingers and hands

Inhale as you open the hands and spread them wide, making big spaces between the fingers.
Exhale as you make fists, closing the fingers over the thumbs and squeezing on the thumbs.
Repeat 5-9 times and then let the hands relax.

Wrists

Circle each wrist 5-9 times in each direction, slowly.
Then circle both wrists 5-9 times in each direction.
Breathe naturally as you do this. Then allow the hands to relax.

Elbows

With the elbows resting on the bed, bend and straighten the arms a few times. *Inhale* as you bend the arms, *exhale* as you straighten them.

Shoulders

Lie with your palms facing up.
Inhale as you draw your shoulders gently towards your ears, keeping your arms relaxed.
Exhale as you draw your shoulders down away from your ears.
Repeat 5-9 times and relax.

Then repeat the exercise, pressing the shoulders down into the bed before you draw them away from the ears.

Toes

Lie with your feet together, toes pointing up.
Inhale and stretch the toes so you make spaces between them (not so hard you give yourself a cramp).
Exhale and curl the toes forward, as if fisting them. Try not to move the ankle, just the toes.
Repeat 5-9 times and let the feet relax before continuing.

Ankles

Inhale as you bend your right foot back at the ankle. Draw the toes back towards you and stretch into the heel.
Exhale as you bend the same foot forward, pointing the toes away.
Do this 5-9 times with each ankle. Then do both ankles together.

Now circle each foot at the ankle, 5-9 times in each direction, breathing naturally. Then circle both ankles together.

Try to keep the rest of the leg still: all the movement should be in the ankle. Let the feet relax when you've finished.

Knees

Lie with your knees bent, your heels close to your buttocks, the soles of the feet resting on the bed.
Inhale as you slide your right foot down the bed, straightening the leg. Press your heel forward.
Exhale as you slide the foot back, bending the leg.
Repeat this 5-9 times. Then do the right knee.

Hips

Lie with your arms relaxed and your legs straight, feet together.
Bend your right knee and place the right foot next to the left ankle.
Inhale as you lower the knee towards the bed. (This will work your right hip – but only if you don't lift the left hip: keep it on the bed!)
Exhale as you bring the knee up.
Do this three times.
Now place the right foot next to the left calf, and repeat the movements.
Then move the right foot next to the left knee, and repeat again.
Then do the movements in all three positions with the left knee bent.

Co-ordinating the movement with the breath makes the movements more effective. It is also both relaxing and energizing, and can help you with any post-operative worries and 'blues'.

Books that Helped

Some people want to know everything there is to know about their disease; some don't. I thought I did, but it seemed that I didn't, at least at first. I was wholly engaged in absorbing the shock of the devastating knowledge I had been given, and in trying to stay clear and steady. I didn't want to know anything other than what was absolutely necessary. I trusted my consultant, accepted his advice, and was grateful to him for moving swiftly to implement it.

So although I began trying to read about cancer when I was first diagnosed, I soon found I couldn't. On nearly every page of every book I opened there was something that threw me into a panic. I was already terrified by the little I knew: I couldn't tolerate any more terror, and I had to stop reading. It was enough for me to take in what was happening to me as it happened, from moment to moment.

I think we need to be aware of the danger of reading too much in the early stages. If you feel out of control, and that gathering as much information as possible as quickly as possible will help you regain control, then read – but know your level of tolerance. Follow your intuition, and if it tells you to shut a book, shut it: don't force yourself to read on. You have enough fears to cope with without deliberately piling on more. If you think you 'should' be gathering information but you can't bear to, trust yourself – it's no reflection on your intelligence – and let the reading wait.

I couldn't and didn't read much at first, but later, during and after my five-month retreat, I was able to tolerate more input and developed an appetite for both information and inspiration. Some of the books I read were disappointing. I've already explained why the ones that exhorted me to maintain a positive attitude and fight my cancer weren't helpful to me. Amongst these I have to include the well-known books by Lawrence Le Shan and Carl and Stephanie Simonton, but I know they have been helpful to others, and I wouldn't want to put anyone off reading them.

Others were useful practically; a few were helpful spiritually. All the ones I liked best were, interestingly, given to me by friends. The following is a short selection of some I have found informative, affirming, encouraging, thought-provoking, uplifting, or a combination of some or all of these.

Death, as Sogyal Rinpoche says in *The Tibetan Book of Living and Dying*, is simply a fact of life: once we accept this, we can truly begin to live. Death is going to arrive for all of us sooner or later: rather than ignore the fact, it's more useful as well as more realistic to accept and prepare for it. This wonderful, lucidly written book, full of humour and spiritual wisdom, tells us how we can do that. Anyone who reads it will be inspired, and guided towards a deeper insight into the meaning of life and death.

Deepak Chopra, an ayurvedic physician, and Bernie Siegel, a surgeon, have each written several good books. I found *Quantum Healing* (Chopra), *Love, Medicine and Miracles* (Siegel) and *Peace, Love and Healing* (Siegel) particularly helpful. These two popular authors, writing for a mass market, have communicated to millions of readers their shared beliefs: that healing begins with a decision to live, a decision that must be made by every cell in one's body; and that serious illness is a profoundly transformative spiritual experience.

Bernie Siegel writes: 'We have biological "live and die" mechanisms within us... the state of mind changes the state of the body by working through the central nervous system, the endocrine system and the immune system.' Through the healing power of love and of trust in God, he says, people can transform, enrich and prolong their lives beyond medical expectation. This outlook is on quite a different level from anything the positive thinking/fight for your life tracts have to offer, and for many people it will be far more helpful.

Audre Lorde, who died in 1992 after surviving breast cancer for 14 years, was an American black lesbian feminist poet. Her short, honest, beautiful book, *The Cancer Journals* is the story of her own journey from despair and anger to acceptance and healing. One of its many strengths is that it addresses the political and environmental issues around the breast cancer epidemic: Audre's grasp of these will help anyone who is struggling with isolating, counter-productive guilt and self-blame to let go of it.

In Audre's forthright discussion of the prosthesis question I found the first echo of my own growing reluctance to wear one, and was confirmed in my eventual decision to be as I am. For that help I am truly grateful, and I recommend *The Cancer Journals* to any woman who may be contemplating doing without a prosthesis, or consigning the one she has been wearing to the back of a cupboard, but who needs a bit of encouragement.

Treya Killam Wilber developed an extremely aggressive form of breast cancer in 1983, and died five years later after a long struggle with metastatic recurrences. In *Grace and Grit: Spirituality and Healing in the Life and Death of Treya Killam Wilber*, her husband, the writer Ken Wilber, has interwoven Treya's journal and his own commentary into a moving portrayal of her courageous struggle for life and equanimity, and her spiritual journey into healing and death. Though not an easy book for me to read, it was ultimately liberating. I read it at a point when I thought I had already faced my own fears squarely and accepted them: it showed me that I hadn't, and it helped me do so.

Grace and Grit also helped me to clarify my views on the nature and causes of illness. For much of what I have said in the chapter 'Please Don't Blame the Victim', I am indebted to Ken's lucid discussion of these issues, which swept my mind clean of confusion.

The title of Chen Yu's *The Rice is Boiled: My Life, My Cancer* refers to a Chinese proverb which says there is nothing one can do to change the rice once it is cooked. It is eaten or it is discarded, and that is life, and we must get on with it! In other words, we need to accept things as they are, life as it is, our illness as it is. Chen Yu is a remarkable woman, a pharmacist, spiritual counsellor and clairvoyant; and this down-to-earth, intelligent and inspiring book is a treasure chest both of practical information and spiritual guidance: a real tonic.

Chen Yu writes: 'Cancer has made me strong because it has drawn me closer and closer to God. Because I now draw on His strength to support me daily I find I am able to live... It is a miracle because this extra life I have been enjoying is God's gift to me and I am trying to use it as I think He would wish me to.' Chen Yu has overturned medical predictions by outliving – a day at a time! – a prognosis of terminal cancer for the past four years. She devotes much of her time to spiritual counselling, especially of cancer patients.

Of the factual books about cancer I have read, I will mention just three.

Breast Cancer: A Guide for Every Woman by Michael Baum, Christobel Saunders and Sheena Meredith, is a completely revised version of Dr Baum's *Breast Cancer: The Facts*, and is a much better, more user-friendly book. It gives full and up-to-date information about all aspects of breast cancer, clearly, concisely and comprehensibly. A major concern of the authors is that despite widespread publicity concerning the importance of breast awareness and early detection of lumps, many women delay reporting symptoms, sometimes for years, for fear of what they might signify. Up to 20 per cent of women present with advanced breast cancer – cancer that has reached the incurable stage, having already spread and formed secondary tumours – when symptoms must already have been detectable for considerable time. The authors' aim has been to present the known facts of breast cancer in such a way as to allay unnecessary fears and anxiety, encourage women to come for help earlier, and help them make informed decisions about treatment.

The Breast Cancer Companion is by Kathy La Tour, an American teacher and journalist who developed breast cancer at the age of 37 and has put together an extremely useful book which covers every aspect of what she calls 'this insane disease'. It weaves together practical information, contributions by experts in every field of cancer treatment and research, and the personal testimony of survivors and their partners.

The book is encouragingly and chattily written and laced with plenty of humour, but it doesn't avoid the big issue. In the Introduction, Kathy writes: 'Coming to an understanding of death is life-affirming work, and when you are ready, it will be the work that takes you to the depths of this disease – a place where true healing can begin. I personally have come to believe that in order to live with this disease, we must struggle with the fact that we could die from it.'

In *Preventing Breast Cancer: The Politics of an Epidemic*, Dr Cathy Read looks at the root causes, which she sees as lying in our diet, environment and social structures. Her book is well researched and comprehensive; one of its strengths is that it identifies some of the vested interests that are such formidable enemies of worthwhile research into prevention. Another is that it goes equally thoroughly into the whole question of breast cancer in the United States and in Britain. Dr Read's description of the success of the American women activists should give heart to women in Britain.

Kat Duff opens *The Alchemy of Illness* with a quote from Virginia Woolf: 'Considering how common illness is, how tremendous the spiritual change that it brings... it becomes strange indeed that it has not taken its place with love and battle and jealousy among the prime themes of literature.' Illness is a universal experience, like death; there is no privilege that can make us immune to its touch, but it offers, if only we can see it that way, an extraordinary vantage point from which to view the terrain of our lives. There is an alchemy at work in illness, a burning away of the dross, and this changes us. Kat Duff's own years of suffering with ME have yielded a profound and fascinating book which draws on psychology, religion, history, anthropology and mythology and changes the way we look at illness.

Finally, Stephen Levine, an American writer and teacher of meditation, who has worked extensively with the dying. I had known of his work for years, but read his books only recently. *Who Dies?*, *Meetings at the Edge*, *Healing into Life and Death*, *A Gradual Awakening*: the titles speak for themselves. They are about healing, meditation, acceptance, forgiveness, love, life, death. Read them when you are ready to, and let them help you open yourself to healing and death and life.

Baum, Michael, Saunders, Christobel, and Meredith, Sheena: *Breast Cancer: A Guide for Every Woman*, Oxford University Press, 1994.

Chopra, Deepak, MD: *Quantum Healing: Exploring the Frontiers of Mind/Body Medicine*, Bantam Books, 1989.

Duff, Kat: *The Alchemy of Illness*, Virago, 1994.

LaTour, Kathy: *The Breast Cancer Companion*, William Morrow and Co, Inc, New York, 1993.

Levine, Stephen: *A Gradual Awakening*, Gateway Books, 1993. *Healing into Life and Death*, Gateway Books, 1989. *Meetings at the Edge: Dialogues with the Grieving and the Dying, the Healing and the Healed*, Gateway Books, 1984. *Who Dies?*, Gateway Books, 1988

Lorde, Audre: *The Cancer Journals*, Sheba Feminist Publishers, 1985.

Read, Dr Cathy: *Breast Cancer: The Politics of an Epidemic*, Harper Collins Publishers, 1995.

Rinpoche, Sogyal: *The Tibetan Book of Living and Dying*, Rider, 1992.

Siegel, Bernie S., MD: *Love, Medicine and Miracles*, Arrow Books, 1986. *Peace, Love and Healing: The Path to Self-Healing*, Arrow Books, 1991 (UK); HarperCollins Publishers Inc, 1989 (US).

Wilber, Ken: *Grace and Grit: Spirituality and Healing in the Life and Death of Treya Killam Wilber*, Shambhala, 1993.

Yu, Chen: *The Rice is Boiled: My Life, My Cancer*, Boyu Publications, 1992.

Notes

Chapter 2
1   Klein, Jean: 'The Great Forgetting' (unpublished article).

Chapter 3
2   Rinpoche, Sogyal: *The Tibetan Book of Living and Dying*, Rider, 1992.
3   Klein, Jean: 'The Great Forgetting'.
4   Noll, Peter: *In the Face of Death*, Penguin Books, 1990.

Chapter 4
5   Siegel, Bernie, MD: *Peace, Love and Healing: The Path to Self-Healing*, Arrow Books, 1993 (UK); HarperCollins Publishers Inc, 1989 (US).
6   Wilber, Ken: *Grace and Grit: Spirituality and Healing in the Life of Treya Killam Wilber*, Shambhala, 1993.
7   Siegel, Bernie, MD: *Peace, Love and Healing: The Path to Self-Healing*, Arrow Books, 1993 (UK); HarperCollins Publishers Inc, 1989 (US).
8   Levine, Stephen: *Healing into Life and Death*, Gateway Books, 1989.

(When parts of this chapter appeared in *Yoga and Health* magazine in the summer of 1994 as 'Reflections on Cancer and Healing', Dr Sandra Goodman, editor of *Health: State of the Art* and *Positive Health*, asked to publish extracts from it in *Positive Health*. She also quoted from it in the *International Journal of Alternative and Complementary Medicine* and in her book *Nutrition and Cancer*, describing it as 'eloquent'. She later wrote to me: 'As you may surmise I read very widely, and yours is the finest refutation I've seen of the dangerous New Age practice of loading blame upon people with cancer.')

Chapter 5
9   Okri, Ben: *African Elegy*, Jonathan Cape, 1992.

10   Siegel, Bernie, MD: *Peace, Love and Healing: The Path to Self-Healing*, Arrow Books, 1993 (UK); HarperCollins Publishers Inc, 1989 (US).

Chapter 6
11   Lorde, Audre: *The Cancer Journals*, Sheba Feminist Publishers, 1985.
12   *ibid.*
13   Read, Dr Cathy: *Preventing Breast Cancer: The Politics of an Epidemic*, Harper Collins Publishers, 1995.
14   Sikora, Professor Karel: 'Breast Cancer – Why Britain's Women Deserve Better', *Reader's Digest*, November 1994

Chapter 8
An audio cassette tape is available with instructions for the breathing exercises in this chapter and the relaxation exercises in Chapter 9. Please write, enclosing cheque or postal order for £7.50 (£8.50 outside the U.K.), to Julie Friedeberger, ℅ Element Books Ltd, Longmead, Shaftesbury, Dorset SP7 8PL.

Chapter 9
15   Harrison, Peter: 'The Great Practice of Breath Awareness', *Dharma Journal*, Winter 1994.

Chapter 10
16   For details of manipulation physiotherapists in your area, contact the Manipulation Association of Chartered Physiotherapists, 14 Bedford Row, London WC1 4ED, telephone 0171 242 1941.

Practical matters
17   The statistics are from 'Cancer Incidence in Five Continents, Volume VI' Parkin, D.M.; Muir C.S.; Whelan S.L.; Gao Y.-T.; Ferlay J.; Powell, J. eds: IARC Scientific Publications No 120, Lyon, 1992.

Useful Addresses

UK

➤ BACUP is the British Association of Cancer United Patients who help patients and families and friends. Trained cancer nurses provide information, emotional support and practical advice by telephone or letter. A range of free publications is available. They also offer a one-to-one counselling service with eight free sessions. 3 Bath Place, Rivington Street, London EC2A 3JR, telephone 0171 613 2121. (Outside London: freephone 0800 181 199.) The telephone number to enquire about counselling is 0171 696 9000.

➤ Breast Cancer Care (formerly Breast Care and Mastectomy Association) offers practical advice, information and support to women concerned about breast cancer. Volunteers who have had breast cancer themselves assist the staff in providing emotional support. They also offer a free fitting service, by appointment, for prostheses, bras and swimwear. 15/19 Britten Street, London SW3 3TZ. Telephone 0171 867 1103 (helpline); 0171 867 8275 (administration).

➤ CancerLink provides emotional support and information on all aspects of cancer. It acts as a resource to cancer support and self-help groups and helps people who set up new groups. 17 Britannia Street, London WV1X 9JN, telephone 0171 833 2451.

➤ The Cancer Relief Macmillan Fund funds training of Macmillan nurses to care for cancer patients in hospital and at home, gives grants to people in financial difficulties because of their illness, and funds medical posts to improve health professionals' knowledge and practice of cancer care. 15/19 Britten Street, London SW3 3TZ, telephone 0171 351 7811.

➤ The Bristol Cancer Help Centre offers a programme of holistic healing, working at the levels of body, mind and spirit. Its aims are to encourage patients to help themselves, to provide a supportive link for cancer patients and their families and friends, and to help patients achieve a better quality of life. The Bristol Centre offers a range of complementary treatments and residential and daytime courses. Grove House, Cornwallis Grove, Clifton, Bristol BS8 4PG, telephone 0117 9743 216.

➤ New Approaches to Cancer encourages awareness of the benefits of holistic healing for cancer patients. It operates a nationwide referral system and information service to guide patients to their nearest source of holistic help. 5 Larksfield, Egham, Surrey TW20 ORB, telephone 01784 433610.

➤ The UK National Breast Cancer Coalition, representing the interests of all women in Britain, are campaigning for a national strategy in the fight to beat breast cancer. If you want to help, write for information to PO Box 8554, London SW8 2ZB.

United States

American Cancer Society
1599 Clifton Road NE
Atlanta, Georgia 30329
Telephone 404 329 7680

Cancer Information Service
Building 31, Room 10A24
National Cancer Institute
Bethesda, Maryland 20892
Telephone 1-800-4-CANCER
1-800-422-6237 (free)

The Cancer Support Community
185 Lundy's Lane
San Francisco, California 94110
Telephone 415 658 9400

Canada

Canadian Cancer Society
Suite 200, 10 Alcorn Avenue
Toronto, Ontario M4V 3B1
Telephone 416 961 7223

Australia

Australian Cancer Society
153 Dowling Street
Woolloomooloo
New South Wales 2011
Telephone 02 358 2066

Quest for Life Foundation
Quest for Life Centre
37 Atchison Street
Crows Nest, New South Wales 2065
or
PO Box 267
Cammeray, New South Wales
Telephone 02 906 3112
Fax 02 906 1203

New Zealand

Cancer Society of New Zealand Inc
Box 12145
Wellington, New Zealand
Telephone 04 4736 409

Printed in the United Kingdom
by Lightning Source UK Ltd.
1420